T0198621

ARE WE SINNERS?

CHRISTIAN AND JEWISH BELIEFS ON SIN AND EVIL

RABBI MICHAEL MAYERSOHN

iUniverse, Inc.
New York   Bloomington

Are We Sinners?

Christian and Jewish Beliefs on Sin and Evil

iUniverse books may be ordered through booksellers or by contacting:

iUniverse
1663 Liberty Drive
Bloomington, IN 47403
www.iuniverse.com
1-800-Authors (1-800-288-4677)

ISBN: 978-1-4401-6911-3 (pbk)
ISBN: 978-1-4401-6912-0 (ebk)

Printed in the United States of America

iUniverse rev. date: 9/30/2009

Table of Contents

Dedication

I happily and proudly dedicate this book, the product of my heart and mind's energies for many years, to my wife, Caryn. She is my comfort, my love and my heart's delight. I also express here my appreciation and gratitude for all my thousands of students over the years, the children and the adults. As the rabbis teach us, "Much have I learned from my teachers but more from my students."

Introduction

You are now embarked upon an intriguing journey, an effort to understand the beliefs and thoughts of historical Judaism and Christianity, as expressed in classical texts, regarding sin and evil. I appreciate your willingness to delve into a fairly serious subject, one that does not lend itself to absolute, concrete truths. The worlds of Jewish and Christian thought on any subject and especially on sin and evil are vast and cannot be defined succinctly or comprehensively. What I will try to do here is explore the basic components of historical teachings, writings and thoughts on the subject, relying on the Hebrew Bible, the rabbinic literature of Talmud and Midrash, Paul in the New Testament, and the writings of Augustine, Thomas Aquinas, and Martin Luther. You the reader will walk away with a basic understanding of what these religious traditions teach about sin and evil. For some, this will be enough and for others it will be the beginning of a deeper exploration.

On a personal note: I am a rabbi, ordained by the seminary of the Reform movement of Judaism, the Hebrew Union College-Jewish Institute of Religion, in 1979. From ordination until 2003 I served as spiritual leader of three Reform congregations in Massachusetts and Southern California. In 2003 I left my congregation to be able to devote most of my time and efforts to teaching Christians about Judaism and the Bible. I established the Alliance for Christian and Jewish Studies to promote and support the classes I have been teaching in Orange County, Greater Long Beach, and San Diego in Southern California and in the Phoenix area in Arizona.

Over the span of several years I immersed myself in academic research into the Jewish doctrine of the evil inclination in the Talmud and Midrash (see an explanation of these and other texts at the end of this Introduction, in the section, "Texts and Sources"). In the translations of Hebrew texts in the book I will refer to the evil inclination by the original Hebrew, *yetzer hara,* and the good inclination by the Hebrew, *yetzer hatov.* In the Talmud and Midrash, the rabbis wrote extensively about their idea of the evil inclination. It is the evil inclination that leads people to commit sins. In teaching about Judaism to Christians I came to realize that while my understanding of the Jewish doctrine of sin and evil was growing and flourishing, my understanding of the Christian doctrine, especially of Original Sin, was woefully inadequate. I thus began, with the guidance of devout, devoted and knowledgeable Christian friends and scholars, to study Christian writings on sin and evil. This book is the result of documentary and personal research, an effort to compare the thought and writings of traditional scholars and sages of Judaism and Christianity on the subject at hand.

My teaching, primarily with Christians about Judaism, specifically about the Jewish context of Jesus' life and words, has expanded greatly over the last few years. I have taught at over twenty-five churches, sometimes coming back to the same church multiple times to teach new classes. I have been profoundly impressed by the eagerness, the enthusiasm, even the hunger, among so many Christians to learn more about the Jewish world in which Jesus lived and taught. People have been keenly interested in learning more about Judaism, including the Judaism of today, the ways in which our respective faith systems are similar and different, and the roots of those similarities and differences. We live in very different times than past generations, in a period of understanding, collaboration, and harmony, and it is good that we acknowledge and appreciate this new reality.

My teaching has expanded beyond the original commitment to teaching about the Jewish context of the beginnings of Christianity, to include extensive teaching of the Hebrew Bible to Christians. I am able to bring the nuances and meaning of the Hebrew text to my classes, exposing people to the subtle plays on words, puns and geo-political components of the Bible. Most of the students are Christians, so this gives me another opportunity to teach Christians about the Jewish understanding of the sacred text. I always point out to my students that my goal is never to identify or pursue a "right" interpretation of the sacred texts but to hold up divergent interpretations so we can understand the cryptic nature of scripture.

In these pages I will examine some fundamental problems that Christianity and Judaism and virtually all people of faith must confront, specifically, the undeniable reality that humans sin. Secular people may have other ways to understand this behavior, but in the religious community when people violate God's expectations and requirements, harming others, engaging in hurtful or illicit sexual relations, or committing needless violence, we understand it to be sin. As people of faith we believe God had at least some responsibility for creating humans. We may or may not believe in the creation story in Genesis, but we accept the premise that God played some role in the existence of the world and of us as humans. And there is the conundrum—how and why would God create humans with the inclination, capacity, or even inevitability of committing sin? What do Jewish and Christian traditional texts identify as the source of our sinful behavior, what leads us to engage in evil deeds? Why couldn't we have simply been created by a loving and merciful God to do only good? What is the meaning of the existence of sin and human evil in a world created by a good and just God?

I will not attempt here to define, in any comprehensive way, sin or evil, relying on an analogy of the Supreme Court's famous definition of pornography: "We know it when we see it." We might all disagree on whether one act or another is sinful, but all of us in the religious community agree that humans commit sin. Now we want to understand what Christianity and Judaism have to say about this problem in their classical texts of antiquity.

The title of the book would seem to presume that we do not know if we are sinners, contradicting what I have just written. The title is intended to ask the religious question of whether we are, according to the faith of Judaism and/or Christianity, inherently sinners, or whether God created us as neutral or good and the sinning is a choice we make in our lives. Are we sinners by our very nature, is sinfulness woven into the very fabric of our being? Did God create us as good and sin is an external corruption of that creation, or did God create us as beings inevitably disposed to sin? And what conclusions flow from our answer to those questions about our constitutional nature as beings created by God?

This book will conclude with a comparison of the different faith systems' views on the topics at hand. Neither system of thought and faith can be defined in monolithic terms, as if there is one Jewish or one Christian idea on sin and evil. I will try to synthesize the ideas and reduce them to digestible and comprehensible schools of thought for each faith tradition. The biblical and rabbinic traditions of Judaism are incredibly diverse and expressive of different ideas on this and myriad other topics. It is in the nature of Judaism not to articulate a unified article of faith on a matter as complex as sin and its origin. Christianity is also a fully developed, rich, and diverse faith tradition and within both Catholicism and Protestantism there exist divergent beliefs and ideas regarding sin and evil. Both in the case of Judaism and Christianity we will examine the dominant and major ideas that have been propounded over the last two thousand years, focusing on primary historical texts, including the Hebrew Bible, New Testament, Talmud, Midrash, writings of Paul, Augustine, Thomas Aquinas, Martin Luther, and more.

Finally, I will compare the two traditions and look at how they are similar and different. My approach to the comparison of Judaism and Christianity is to acknowledge points of commonality and areas of divergence and not try to paper over, diminish, or resolve the differences. We learn to live together, even love each other, not by pretending we are the same, but by acknowledging what we share, respecting what separates and distinguishes us, and loving each other despite the differences.

Texts and Sources

As I mentioned above, the Jewish sources for this book are the Hebrew Bible, Talmud and Midrash. The Bible is a collection of books written over a period of nearly a thousand years, expressing divergent views on many ideas and concepts, especially something as fundamental as sin and evil. In this book I will take the view that the Bible was written by many human authors. The Bible as we have it began as an oral tradition and was ultimately written down by numerous scribes and writers. While some may debate the role of God in the creation of the text, for our purposes here we will treat it as a text of human creation, reflecting the thinking and beliefs of its human creators.

The rabbinic literature, Talmud and Midrash, are not single books but a result of a creative process that took place over several centuries. The process of creating Talmud began in 100 CE[1] and ended with its redaction in around 500 CE. The Talmud consists of sixty-three volumes of the discussions, debates and discourses in Babylonian and Palestinian rabbinic academies.[2] Over the span of these four centuries, scribes took notes of the discussions, then organized the notes topically and edited them into the sixty-three volumes. In the Talmud text the rabbis discuss every imaginable life issue and concern, among them the inclination humans have to transgress God's commandments. They called this inclination the *yetzer hara*, or evil inclination. In the body of the paper I will refer to the evil inclination and in the rabbinic texts I will leave it untranslated as the *yetzer hara.*

The Midrash was created over approximately the same period as the Talmud, although extending into the ninth century CE. There are several collections of Midrash and the text has a different focus than Talmud. Where the Talmud typically, although not always, focuses on Jewish practice and law, the Midrash includes stories, teachings, sermons and legends. In the Midrash the rabbis attempt to elucidate their view on Biblical texts, often in sermonic form, and express their interpretation of those texts. Both Talmud and Midrash are vast bodies of literature covering virtually every aspect of the human experience.

When we consider the beliefs, opinions, and attitudes of the rabbis in Talmud and Midrash we should always recognize that there is rarely a unified, systematic approach. Different rabbis in different times and texts will articulate different views and in some cases those views will conflict with each other. The characteristic diversity of views contained in rabbinic literature reflects the nature of Jewish life throughout history—a tolerance, even an embrace of diversity and complexity. This is the case with the evil inclination and the capacity for sin as much as any other articles of faith in rabbinic literature. In my discussion here of the rabbinic view of the evil inclination I will acknowledge areas of consensus, and will identify cases where only one belief is expressed and where there are multiple perspectives.

The Christian sources begin with the New Testament, focusing on Paul's writings on sin. While Bible scholars will argue and dispute whether Paul wrote all the texts ascribed to him, we will operate on the premise that if a text is ascribed to Paul, it was written by Paul. His career and writing spanned the years soon after the death of Jesus in the early 30s of the first century CE to his death in the mid-60s.

We will continue our examination of Christian writings with those of St. Augustine of N. Africa. Augustine lived from 354-430 CE and is generally understood to be the preeminent theologian of the early

Church. There are, of course, many people since the fifth century who dispute or even reject some or much of Augustine's writings and ideas, but any examination of early Christian thought has to include his work. We will most closely examine his writings on the subject of sin and evil in *Confessions* and the *City of God*. Our examination of Christian writings and thought on sin and evil will continue after the time of Augustine. We will examine the writings of Thomas Aquinas, the thirteenth century Italian theologian so important to medieval Christian thought, and Martin Luther, the initiator of the Protestant Reformation in the sixteenth century. We will conclude with a brief look at Vatican II in the 1960s.

There is no way, in a concise, accessible book like this to be completely exhaustive of Christian or Jewish writings on the subject at hand. I have therefore restricted the scope of the book to Bible, Talmud and Midrash for Jewish writings and to Paul in the New Testament, Augustine, Aquinas and Martin Luther and Vatican II for the Christian world. One can easily cite teachings of both traditions that are not contained in this volume and point out that one teaching or another is not included in these pages. This book is not intended to be exhaustive of every teaching of Judaism or Christianity. We will explore the seminal texts of the respective traditions to provide the reader with a thorough, if not entirely comprehensive overview of the thinking of these faith traditions concerning sin and human evil.

1. Dates throughout the book will use the convention common in Jewish historical writings and becoming more common in Christian academic writing as well. All dates will use the conventional numbers, but instead of BC and AD, referring to the life and divinity of Jesus, we will use BCE and CE—Before the Common Era and the Common Era. This convention is more inclusive than the traditional terms.

2. There are some references in the book from the Jerusalem, or Palestinian Talmud. This rabbinic document was created in rabbinic academies in Palestine and is substantially from the same period as the Babylonian Talmud. It is considered to be of relatively minor importance. When I refer here to the Talmud without qualification, I am always referring to the Babylonian Talmud.

CHAPTER 1   SIN IN THE HEBREW BIBLE

We find numerous references to sin in the Bible and a few in-depth discourses on the nature of sin, what constitutes sin, how one repents and whether God forgives our sins. Sin and God's response to it are prevailing themes of the sacred text as we return to the ideas again and again. Sin is the primary source of human and divine conflict and drama. Sin creates conflict in human interaction and in our relationship with God. The interplay of sin and repentance provides the push and pull of the human connection with God. Sin drives us away when we transgress and repentance draws us close to God when we turn away and return to God's ways.

In this chapter we will examine the Bible's references to and discussions of sin in an attempt to understand what the Biblical text sees as specific sins, the process of atonement and forgiveness and the large category of sacrificial sin offerings. We will also examine the most extensive Biblical discourse on sin, Solomon's prayer as recorded in I Kings 8. The goal will be to understand how the Biblical writer understood and conceived of human and specifically Israelite sinfulness and how it affects our relationship to God.

Very near the beginning of the Bible we read a declarative statement about sin that lays the groundwork for much of the later Jewish traditional understanding of human sin and the ability of people to control and manage sinful impulses. God is speaking to Adam and Eve's oldest son, Cain, in the wake of his distress at realizing that God was paying heed to his brother Abel's sacrifices and not to Cain's. Responding to Cain's distress, God says to him, "Surely if you do right there is uplift. But if you do not do right sin couches at the door; its urge is toward you, yet you can be its master." (Genesis 4:7) This is the first place in the Hebrew Bible where we see the word sin and it is worth noting that it is in the context of contentious feelings that lead to an act of violence. The expression, "sin couches at the door," suggests that sin is ever present, waiting to take advantage of a person's inclination to let it in. The close and looming presence of sin tells us that we are likely to succumb in any moment and that it is seductive and enticing. Sin is right there, "at the door," through which one has to pass to be part of the world. But while "its urge is toward you," each person has the power to rule over sin and master it. Sin is personified as having an urge and that urge is toward the person with feelings of exclusion, rejection and anger. From this first explicit reference to sin in the Hebrew Bible the sacred text is teaching that sin lurks nearby, that it is not passive but active, and that it cannot be defeated or vanquished, and can only be managed and controlled.

These themes, that sin is always near and present, that it possesses a desire toward humans and that people can control and manage it, are stressed repeatedly in the later rabbinic tradition, as we will see in subsequent chapters. God's statement to Cain is quoted frequently in the rabbinic literature to support the idea that sin is not something that is alien to people or of passing interest, but that it is close, seductive and persistent.

The Christian reader may perceive something missing from this initial discussion of sin in the Bible. We jumped right to the story of Cain and Abel, ignoring the story of Adam and Eve and the violation of God's commandment not to eat the fruit of the tree of knowledge of good and evil. As we will see in the later discussion of the Christian tradition and the idea of Original Sin, this story is the very foundation of Christian teaching on the subject. Jewish tradition never focuses on the Adam and Eve story in the context of sin and the word sin is not used in the telling of the story. This is the beginning of the differences between Judaism and Christianity on the question of sin and its place in human behavior.

At the end of the Noah Flood story in Genesis, after the waters have receded and everyone has exited the ark, Noah builds an altar and makes sacrificial offerings to God. God is depicted as being pleased by the sacrifice and "said to Himself, 'Never again will I doom the earth because of man, since the devisings of man's mind are evil from his youth; nor will I ever again destroy every living being as I have done.'" (Genesis 8:20f) After destroying all of the living beings on earth because of their wickedness, God resolves never to do that again while acknowledging that man has the capacity for evil "from his youth." This suggests, as later rabbinic texts that we will examine in subsequent chapters will describe, that the evil inclination of humans is there from the beginning. Humans have this capacity not because of something they learn along the way or because of life experiences, but because that is how they were designed. This will have immense importance both for the rabbinic tradition in their discussion of the good and evil inclination and certainly for Christianity and its consideration of the idea of Original Sin.

In numerous instances in the Bible the references to sin are unspecific and undefined. The listener and reader are left to guess or deduce what constitutes sin, or it is assumed that they will understand what the sin is. Before we read about the outrageous acts of the men of Sodom and Gomorrah (Genesis 19), God is depicted as speculating on whether to talk to Abraham about the plan to destroy the cities.

God is quoted as thinking, "The outrage of Sodom and Gomorrah is so great, and their sin so grave!" (Genesis 18:20) The reader is left to wonder what their sin is, and after reading Genesis 19 and the story of the crude people of Sodom one is still left guessing whether the sin is the homosexual brutality of the men or their inhospitable treatment of the visitors. God identifies their sin as grave, but the reader is not explicitly told what the sin is. Jewish tradition holds that the sin of the people is their threatened violence against the guests as suggested by Lot's offer of his daughters in their stead. Lot's plea on their behalf is based on his responsibility to take care of them when he says, "do not do anything to these men, since they have come under the shelter of my roof." (Genesis 19:8) In Ezekiel (16:49-50) we read of Sodom, "pride, fulness of bread, and careless ease was in her and in her daughters; neither did she strengthen the hand of the poor and needy. And they were haughty." It was their arrogance and insensitivity, especially in the face of their own material comfort, that constituted their sin.

Several key figures in the Torah ask a question, apparently rhetorically, regarding a sin they might have committed. When Laban, Jacob's father-in-law, is pursuing him after Jacob had fled his household, Jacob asks, "What is my transgression, how have I sinned that you should pursue me?" (Genesis 31:36) Similarly, Joseph, in the wake of the alleged seduction of Potiphar's wife, asks, "How could I do this most wicked thing, and sin before God?" (Genesis 39:9) Reuben, one of Jacob's twelve sons, rebukes his brothers for their abduction and sale of Joseph, asking, "Did I not tell you, 'Do not sin against the boy?'" (Genesis 42:22) The speaker always knows the answer to his question. There was a shared understanding of what constituted sin and the presumption that sin could have been avoided and that the person who chooses to sin is held accountable for his transgression.

We frequently read of people sinning in the Biblical text, especially in the narratives of Genesis and Exodus, with warnings against sinning and without any clear or obvious definition of what the sin is. The reader is left to assume or understand what the sin under question is, what the speaker has in mind. In the concluding passages of the Joseph epic in Genesis, the brothers claim to quote their father Jacob in urging Joseph not to seek retribution: "Forgive the sin of your brothers who treated you so harshly." (Genesis 50:17) The listener/reader wonders whether the harsh treatment of Joseph by the brothers was the sin or whether something more specific, like their lying about his fate or selling him into slavery constituted the sin.

After the seventh plague inflicted on Pharoah and the Egyptians, after Pharoah repeatedly recanted his permission to the Israelites to go into the wilderness to serve God, we read that Pharoah "became stubborn and continued to sin." (Exodus 9:34) We are left to assume that it was his defiance of God, his refusal to let the Israelites go that was his sin, but it is possible that the reference to his continuing to sin is a more general message about his lifestyle and leadership. Pharoah himself pleads to be forgiven of his sins, using the same simple phrase that King David will use when confronted by Nathan after his sexual violation of Bat Sheva: "*Chatati l'Adonai,*" "I have sinned before Adonai." (Exodus 10:16; David in II Samuel 12:13) It is a simple and profound acknowledgment of sinful behavior without explanation or justification.

The prophets offer broad condemnations of the people for their sinful behavior and at times we have to deduce from the context what sin they are talking about. Isaiah forcefully declares, "Be your sins like crimson, they can turn snow-white; be they red as dyed wool, they can become like fleece." (Isaiah 1:18) This speaks to the possibility of forgiveness for the sin and only from the context of the preceding verses can we conclude that the sin of which Isaiah is speaking is social injustice. Again in a very generalized way, referring to a broad understanding of sinful behavior Isaiah declares, "Ah, those who haul sin with cords of falsehood and iniquity as with cart ropes." (Isaiah 5:18) Without cataloging the particulars the prophet establishes that mere defiance of God constitutes sin, "Oh, disloyal sons declares the Lord. Making plans against my wishes, weaving schemes against My will, thereby piling sin upon sin." (Isaiah 30:1) While there is great debate between Christian and Jewish tradition regarding the identity of the servant in Isaiah 53, he seems to bear the sins of others, "My righteous servant makes the many righteous, it is their punishment that he bears…he was numbered among the sinners, whereas he bore the sin of many and made intercession for sinners." (Isaiah 53:11f)

Unspecified sin can trap a person and bring reproach to a people (Proverbs 5:22, 14:34) and we read that Job did not sin against God even after experiencing unspeakable suffering at God's hand (Job 1:22). In the many instances where the Bible does not specify the sin under consideration the presumption appears to be that the reader knows what sin is.

The text does exhaustively and comprehensively recount the sins of the Israelites, the sins God condemns. Numerous specific acts and categories of behavior are identified in the Bible as sins and the people are warned about them, cautioned to avoid them. There is an understanding that other nations will lead the Israelites to sin and that the sinful behavior of other nations has to be avoided. God tells the people that the inhabitants of the Land of Israel will not remain in the land so that they cannot lead the Israelites to sin (Exodus 20:17). The land becomes corrupted as a result of the sinful behavior of the inhabitants:

> Thus the land itself became defiled;
> and I (God) called it to account for
> its iniquity, and the land spewed out
> its inhabitants. But you must keep
> My laws and My rules, and you must
> not do any of those abhorrent things,
> neither the citizen nor the stranger
> who resides among you. For all those
> abhorrent things were done by the
> people who were in the land before
> you, and the land became defiled.

So let not the land spew you out for
defiling it, as it spewed out the nation
that came before you.[1]

The Israelites are cautioned against many specific acts that are
identified as sins. Blaspheming God (Leviticus 24:15), violation of a
vow (Deuteronomy 23:23), abusing a needy laborer and withholding
his pay (Deuteronomy 24:15) are all defined as sinful behavior. As we
saw in Isaiah (1:17f) and elsewhere (Deuteronomy 15:9), acts of social
injustice are sins. The tribes of Gad and Reuben are told that their
reluctance to enter the Land of Israel with the other tribes, their interest
in staying on the east bank of the Jordan River is sinful. Cheating in
business practices is identified as a sin (Proverbs 20:9f) and robbing
one's parents is a sin (Proverbs 28:24). In one instance the sin of
the Israelites in the wilderness was not the Golden Calf (see below)
but the defiance of the Israelites when they demanded better food,
rejecting God's nurturance and providence (Psalms 78:17f). Making
vows one will not or cannot keep is a case of the mouth leading a
person to sin (Ecclesiastes 5:5). In general, any time a person acts
contrary to the commands, expectations and desires of God, rebelling
against God's word, the Bible identifies the behavior as sinful. We are
in relationship with God and with each other and whenever we violate
either relationship, either with acts that defy God or acts that wrong
another person, we have sinned.

In several instances Biblical figures identify their own sins or they
are identified for them. Aaron acknowledges that the criticism that
he and Miriam launched against Moses, challenging his position of
leadership, was a sin (Numbers 12:11). The sons of the priest Eli are
described as scoundrels (I Samuel 2:12) and their sin is defined rather
broadly as having "treated the Lord's offerings impiously." (I Samuel
2:17) Samuel lets Saul know that his sins are numerous, "For rebellion
is like the sin of divination, defiance like the iniquity of teraphim
(idols); because you rejected the Lord's command, He has rejected you
as king." (I Samuel 15:23) In the Psalms, we read that the Israelites'

sin against God in the wilderness was not restricted to the creation and worship of the golden calf. Their lack of faith in God as demonstrated in their whining about the food was also a sin: "They went on sinning against Him, defying the Most High in the parched land. To test God was in their mind when they demanded food for themselves. They spoke against God, saying, 'Can God spread a feast in the wilderness?'" (Psalms 78:17)

The greatest single instance of Israelite sin, the event that is referred to several times throughout the Bible and the rabbinic literature as the greatest example of sin, is the incident of the Israelites' creation and worship of the Golden Calf in the wilderness. When Moses learns about the act of idolatry he turns to Aaron and asks, "What did this people do to you that you have brought such great sin upon them?" (Exodus 32:21) Moses reminds the people of the Golden Calf sin, recounting the event, "I saw how you had sinned against the Lord your God: you had made yourselves a molten calf; you had been quick to stray from the path that the Lord had enjoined upon you." (Deuteronomy 9:16) Moses recalls his own response to the terrible sin, "As for that sinful thing you had made, the calf, I took it and put it to the fire; I broke it to bits and ground it thoroughly until it was fine as dust, and I threw its dust into the brook that comes down the mountain." (Deuteronomy 9:21) Moses recounts his prayer to God, interceding once again on the people's behalf, this time because of their sin of the Golden Calf, "Give thought to Your servants, Abraham, Isaac and Jacob, and pay no heed to the stubbornness of this people, its wickedness, its sinfulness." (Deuteronomy 9:27)

This incident of ultimate sinful rebellion against God, a rejection of God, becomes the reference point for any leader or prophet who seeks to remind the people of their inclination to sin. The prophet Hosea refers to Israel sinning by making molten images and idols, "They are wont to kiss calves." (Hosea 13:2) There is a veiled reference to the incident in Jeremiah, when the people ask God what their sin is and God responds, "Because your fathers deserted me…and followed other gods and served them and worshiped them; they deserted Me and did not keep my Torah." (Jeremiah 16:10, 18) Idolatry generally and the incident of the Golden Calf specifically, is the greatest example of sin that an Israelite can commit.

Jeroboam, king of the northern kingdom of Israel after the reign of Solomon, sought to avoid having the Israelites make pilgrimage to Judea in the south where they might become loyal to his adversary, King Rehoboam. To keep the Israelites home he "made two golden calves. He said to the people, 'You have been going up to Jerusalem long enough. This is your god, O Israel, who brought you up from the land of Egypt!" (I Kings 12:28) The words at the end of the verse exactly repeat the words the Israelites offered at the creation of the golden calf in the wilderness.[2] This incident is the low point of Jeroboam's reign and leads to the observation of the prophet Ahijah, "You have acted worse than all those who preceded you; you have gone and made for yourself other gods and molten images to vex Me." (I Kings 14:9) The sin of idolatry, and especially this worship of the emblematic golden calf, is the great sin of the Israelites.

Several of the Israelite kings sin against God, especially in the practice or tolerance of idolatry. From Solomon to Manasseh kings import and endorse the worship of idols, the building of shrines and sacred pillars, and engage in rejection of God's teachings prohibiting idolatry. Led by these kings the Israelites fall into a pattern of sinful rebellion against God followed by repentance and return to God and then a repeat of the pattern all over again.

The prophets vehemently condemn the Israelite practice of idolatry, making clear they see it as a rejection of God and the ultimate instance of unacceptable behavior. Isaiah depicts idolatry as a sin when he pleads to Israel to cease their transgression, "Return, O children of Israel, to Him to whom they have been so shamefully false; for in that day everyone will reject his idols of silver and idols of gold, which your hands have made a sin." (Isaiah 31:6) Jeremiah rails against the sinful acts of the Israelites, referring to the idolatrous structures, "Because of the sin of your shrines throughout your borders, I will make your rampart a heap in the field and all your treasures a spoil." (Jeremiah 17:3)

Punishment for sin can be terrifying and final: "If a man's sin is a capital offense and he is put to death, you shall impale him on a stake." (Deuteronomy 21:22) But each person is only punished for his own sins, not for those of one's parents or children, "Parents shall not be put to death for children, nor children be put to death for parents; a person shall only be put to death for his own sin." (Deuteronomy 24:16) The prophet Ezekiel lays out a formulation of sin and punishment that makes it clear we are punished for our own sins. Previous deeds, righteous or evil, are irrelevant in deciding whether we will be punished for what we are doing now: "The righteousness of the righteous will not save him when he sins, nor shall the wickedness of the wicked cause him to stumble when he turns back from his wickedness. The righteous shall not survive through his righteousness when he sins." (Ezekiel 33:12f)

In Leviticus we read about the various sacrificial offerings the people were commanded to make in order to maintain, restore, and repair their relationship with God after committing a sin. The five primary offerings are burnt, grain, peace, sin, and guilt; there is the additional offering specifically for the ordination of priests. Each offering has its specific ritual and purpose. The variations on sin offerings in Leviticus 4 include the case of the person who sins unintentionally, violating God's commandments prohibiting unspecified acts. It can be the priest, the whole community, a chieftain or a common person who commits the unintentional sin. In each case the offending sinner can make an offering to atone for his transgression.

The guilt offering spelled out in Leviticus 5 addresses cases of a person knowingly violating a commandment, specifically if he does not offer exculpatory evidence for someone else, if he touches an impure object or if he makes an oath "to good or bad purpose." (Leviticus 5:4)

In addition to making the sacrificial offering the person who sinned has to confess his guilt. Regarding sins committed against an individual, in which one has inflicted losses on another person because he has been deceitful, fraudulent or has sworn falsely, the transgressor must restore the person's losses plus a penalty of one-fifth the value of what was lost. (Leviticus 5:20ff) After restoration he then has to make the guilt offering.[3]

When a person sins, whether unwittingly or on purpose and whether it has caused a loss to a person or not, he has ruptured his relationship with God. In some cases there must be a confession, in the hope of some restoration, but in all cases the one who has sinned has to offer a sacrifice as a way of restoring the relationship with God. Sinful acts, whether on purpose or accidental, whether they are a violation of God's explicit commandments or causing harm to another person or both, create distance between the sinner and God. The offering, in addition to whatever other acts are required, diminishes that distance.

We have one clear case in the Bible of a person offering a prayerful confession of his own sins and that of his people. Daniel offers a prayer that continues, in part, to be included in Jewish liturgy for the High Holy Days, a time of repentance for sin. We read that he turns his face to God and offers this prayer:

> O Lord, great and awesome God,
> who stays faithful to His covenant
> with those who love Him and keep
> his commandments! We have sinned;
> we have gone astray; we have acted
> wickedly; we have been rebellious
> and have deviated from Your
> commandments and Your rules, and
> have not obeyed Your servants the
> prophets who spoke in Your name
> to our kings, our officers, our father,
> and all the people of the land...The

shame, O Lord, is on us, on our kings,
our officers, and our fathers, because
we have sinned against You. To the
Lord our God belong mercy and
forgiveness, for we rebelled against
Him, and did not obey the Lord our
God by following His teachings that
He set before us through His servants
the prophets....I was speaking,
praying, and confessing my sin and
the sin of my people Israel, and laying
my supplication before the Lord my
God on behalf of the holy mountain
of my God.[4]

Setting the tone of thousands of years of Jewish repentance, Daniel
offers it in the first person plural, acknowledging that the sinner is part
of a community in which people sin and we bear responsibility for each
other. In an entirely different context, Saul also acknowledges his sin
and confesses, but he confesses to Samuel and Samuel does not offer
him any hope of forgiveness.

Moses tries to make a deal with God to "win forgiveness for [their]
sin." (Exodus 32:30). He tells them they have been guilty of a great
sin in the incident of the golden calf and that he will approach God
on their behalf. In seeking God's forgiveness Moses starts with the
acknowledgment that they have sinned and tells God either to forgive
them or remove him "from the record You have written." (Exodus
32:32) God responds rather vaguely that He will only erase from the
record those who have sinned, never indicating whether he forgives
the people. We see a much more clear, systematic expression of the
theology of God's forgiveness in the wake of having written two new
tablets of the commandments for Moses. God passed before Moses and
said:

> The Lord! The Lord!—a God
> compassionate and gracious, slow to
> anger, abounding in kindness and
> faithfulness, extending kindness to
> the thousandth generation, forgiving
> iniquity, transgression and sin; yet
> He does not remit all punishment,
> but visits the iniquity of parents upon
> children and children's children, upon
> the third and fourth generation.[5]

God takes a balanced posture toward sin, forgiveness and punishment; God is tremendously patient and inclined to forgiveness but does punish sin and the punishment can continue for generations. This last idea would appear to be a contradiction of the Deuteronomy 24:16 verse cited above, where we read that a person will only be put to death for his own sins, not those of parents or children. The distinction seems to be that in Deuteronomy we are hearing about a punishment of death and here in Exodus we are reading about forgiveness of sin and presumably a punishment short of death.[6]

Forgiveness of sin is a topic the Bible returns to again and again as people express their hope, expectation and yearning for forgiveness. Saul seeks forgiveness from Samuel for his sin in defying God's commandments. (I Samuel 15:25) In Isaiah we read of a seraph (mythical figure sometimes understood to be an angel) who "flew over to me with a live coal, which he had taken from the altar with a pair of tongs. He touched it to my lips and declared, 'Now that this has touched your lips, Your guilt shall depart and your sin be purged away.'" (Isaiah 6:7) Israel's sins are forgiven as a result of the destruction of idolatrous shrines, altars and sacred posts. (Isaiah 27:9) Jeremiah becomes so angry with the people for their rejection of his prophecy that he pleads with God not to forgive them their sins, "O Lord, You know all their plots to kill me. Do not pardon their iniquity, do not blot out their guilt from Your presence." (Jeremiah 18:23) God describes a time in the future when the people will no longer rebel against God, when they will heed God's words and God will "forgive their iniquities and remember their sins no more." (Jeremiah 31:34)

The primary tasks of the prophet are to warn the people to stop sinful behavior, to caution them about the impending punishment, to urge them to return to God. Ezekiel is told quite explicitly that he is a "watchman for the House of Israel," (Ezekiel 3:17) and that his job is to receive God's word and transmit it to the people. If a wicked man is not warned of his punishment by the prophet the man will die and God will "require a reckoning for his blood from you (the prophet)." (Ezekiel 3:18) If the prophet does warn the man and he persists in his sin, then it is his problem. God goes on in this passage to tell Ezekiel that a righteous man who stumbles and sins will not be favored because of past righteousness and he will pay for his sin and the prophet will again be liable if he has not warned the man. The prophet clearly has a tremendous responsibility to warn people not to sin and if he does not and a person sins, the person is still liable for his sin and the prophet is responsible for the transgression of failing to warn him. The prophet bears great responsibility if he fails to warn people not to sin and they subsequently sin.

There is assurance that God will forgive people their sins if they repent and change their ways. We read that God "will forgive Your people's iniquity, pardon all their sins; You will withdraw all Your anger, turn away from Your rage." (Psalms 85:3) A person can admit to having sinned and repent and expect forgiveness: "I acknowledged my sin to You; I did not cover up my guilt; I resolved, 'I will confess my transgressions to the Lord,' and You forgave the guilt of my sin." (Psalms 32:5) In fact it brings a person happiness to achieve forgiveness for sin: "Happy is he whose transgression is forgiven, whose sin is covered over." (Psalms 32:1) Conversely, it will be disturbing to live with sin that is not forgiven: "There is no soundness in my flesh because of Your rage, no wholeness in my bones because of my sin." (Psalms 38:4)

In all the Biblical sources cited so far, we have seen isolated verses or passages talking about what constitutes sin, how we atone for sin and the nature of God's forgiveness. The discussions of sin offerings in Leviticus and Numbers are one of only two places where we have anything approaching a systematic discourse on a subject relating to sin. The second instance of a comprehensive, systematic discourse on sin is when King Solomon, in his prayer to God at the time of the triumphal arrival of the Ark of the Covenant to the new Temple, offers a lengthy prayer. He begins the remarkable prayer with an invocation of God's promise to his father, David, expressing the hope that the promise of being able to build the Temple, the House of God, will be fulfilled through him, Solomon. He articulates his hope that God will look favorably on Solomon and the House he has built as God's dwelling place. He continues with a discourse offering his hope that God will forgive the people for their sins:

> Should the heavens be shut up and
> there be no rain, because they have
> sinned against You, and then they pray
> toward this place and acknowledge
> Your name and repent of their sins,
> when You answer them, oh, hear in
> heaven and pardon the sin of Your
> servants, Your people Israel, after
> You have shown them the proper
> way in which they are to walk; and
> send down rain upon the land which
> You have to Your people as their
> heritage....In any plague and in any
> disease, in any prayer or supplication
> offered by any person among all Your
> people Israel—each of whom knows
> his own affliction—when he spreads
> his palms toward this House, oh, hear
> in Your heavenly abode, and pardon
> and take action! Render to each man

according to his ways as You know his
heart to be—for You alone know the
hearts of all men....When they sin
against You—for there is no man who
does not sin...and they turn back to
You with all their heart and soul,...
oh, give heed in Your heavenly abode
to their prayer and supplication,
uphold their cause, and pardon Your
people who have sinned against You
for all the transgressions that they have
committed against You...and may You
heed them whenever they call upon
You. For You, O Lord God, have set
them apart for Yourself from all the
peoples of the earth as Your very own,
as You promised through Moses Your
servant when You freed our fathers
from Egypt.[7]

In this amazing prayer, the singular personal and extensive prayer
in the Hebrew Bible, Solomon lays out a theological foundation for
sin and expectations of God's forgiveness. He states that drought and
other calamities are God's punishment for the people's sins and he
expects the people will eventually repent of their sins. He declares
that everyone sins and therefore everyone needs God's forgiveness. It
is God's responsibility to show the people the proper path for their
behavior and Solomon hopes and expects that when they repent for
their sins, God will forgive them. He pleads for God's forgiveness and
bases that hope at least in part on the fact that God has "set them
apart for Yourself from all the peoples of the earth as Your very own."
Solomon's poignant yearning for God's forgiveness of the people is
striking and there is the implication that as the leader of the people the
king is uniquely positioned to make that request. He knows the people
will sin and fervently hopes that God will, having selected them out

from all the other peoples, choose to pardon them of their sins.

The Hebrew Bible, in its various references to sin and forgiveness and especially in Solomon's and Daniel's prayers, offers an understanding of what sin is, how people can repent for it and the hope and expectation that God will forgive the people's sins. We learn that sin is a temptation to every person, even from youth, and that it is a potential snare throughout a person's life. Idolatry, especially as demonstrated in the infamous incident of the Golden Calf, is the most troubling and recurring concern of the Bible's focus on sin. The transgression of social injustice, treating the vulnerable badly, is a second great sin identified by the prophets. The Bible lays out detailed instructions for atoning for sin through sacrifices, repentance and confession. The Biblical text offers the view that sin is a common element of the human experience and that its temptation is great. In offering the path to seeking forgiveness the sacred scripture expresses the yearning and expectation that God will forgive people's sin. We depend on God's unbounded mercifulness, God's inclination to forgive us, since it is seemingly inevitable we will sin and without God's forgiveness we will suffer terribly as a consequence. The Bible does not articulate a view on why people sin, how this inclination becomes universal to the human experience or what the origin of sin is. That will come from the subsequent rabbinic literature.

1. Leviticus 18:25-28

2. The difference between the two statements is in the Hebrew: in Exodus the Israelites say "Eleh Elohecha," suggesting the statement in the plural, "These are your gods." In I Kings the first words are, "Hinei Elohecha," which can be translated in singular or plural. This is ironic since in Exodus they apparently created one calf and Jeroboam clearly

created two. Jeroboam's creation of two calves, coupled with the plural language in Exodus leads to the conclusion that the Israelites actually created two calves in the wilderness, not one.

3. The laws of sin and guilt offerings in Leviticus are replicated with great similarity but with much less detail in Numbers 15 and 18.

4. Daniel 9:4ff

5. Exodus 34:6f

6. We could also take the view that two separate passages dealing with the same subject, here regarding sin and punishment, need not be reconciled, but can be understood as reflecting the views of two distinct authors. Two conflicting views merely reflect different beliefs about God and forgiveness.

7. I Kings 8:35ff

CHAPTER 2   THE ORIGIN AND ULTIMATE DISPOSITION OF THE EVIL INCLINATION IN RABBINIC LITERATURE

Humans have an incredible capacity for sinful behavior, for acting contrary to the wishes of God, and this capacity seems to be universal, persistent and durable. The rabbis of the ancient world[1] contend with this phenomenon and reach conclusions about the origin of the evil inclination at the beginning of life and its fate in the world to come.[2] Since they posit a God of goodness Who created the world and humans, they have to explain how such a phenomenon as human sinfulness can even exist. How can humans be so constituted that virtually all would at least consider sinful and ungodly behavior? The answer of the rabbis is that God created human beings with this capacity, that this common rejection of God's commandments is, in fact, part of God's creative plan and design for humans. The evil inclination is not a corruption of the human spirit or some result of deterioration of basic human goodness over time, but the way God created man.

The rabbis depict God in one instance speaking of regret for having created the evil inclination in man:

> It was a regrettable error on My part
> to have created a *yetzer hara* within
> him, for had I not created a *yetzer hara*
> within him he would not have rebelled
> against Me.[3]

While this text holds that the implantation of the evil inclination in humans was a regrettable error on God's part, other texts agree that God implanted the inclination but contend that it turns out ultimately to be a good or at least necessary thing:

> 'Behold, it was good,' (Genesis 1:31)
> refers to the good inclination. 'And
> behold, it was very good,' refers to
> the evil inclination. Can then the
> evil inclination be very good? That
> would be remarkable! But for the evil
> inclination, however, no man would
> build a house, take a wife and have
> children.[4]

This text is typically seen in Jewish tradition as the classical source for understanding the rabbinic view of the evil inclination. Here the rabbis articulate the belief that God created man with the evil inclination because without it man would not engage in the creative, acquisitive and sexual behavior that is necessary to the human condition. It is the belief of the rabbis that God created man with an evil inclination because it is that very capacity that compels humans to act fully as humans. God intended humans to behave under the influence of the evil inclination, to live with that challenge of combatting the urges of the evil inclination. The evil inclination can be compared to fire—it can be destructive, even fatal, but it is necessary for the perpetuation of human life.

Not only did God create both a good inclination and an evil inclination, making both essential to the human spirit, but we are commanded to acknowledge the benefit of having an evil inclination. As we just saw, the evil inclination leads people to create homes, marry and procreate, making it necessary and even good. Therefore it is deserving of blessing:

> It is incumbent on a man to bless
> [God] for the evil in the same way as
> for the good, as it says, "And you shall
> love the Lord your God with all your
> heart." (Deuteronomy 6:5) "With
> all your heart" means with your two
> inclinations, the evil inclination as
> well as the good inclination.[5]

God's creation of man with an evil inclination becomes a two-edged sword, as the same character composition that leads people to achieve, acquire and procreate is the character that leads them to sin. The rabbis understand that because God created us with this inclination to sin, people will have an opening to blame God for their sinful behavior. In one Midrash text, the rabbis depict the Israelites as protesting to God that they are the clay and God is the potter and any imperfection in their form, i.e. the evil inclination, is the responsibility of the potter, not the clay.[6] Relying on a verse from the Torah frequently cited by the rabbis in this context, Genesis 8:21, "The imagination of man's heart is evil from his youth," the rabbis argue that God created us with the inclination to sin. The rabbis depict the Israelites as pleading for mercy and relief from the burden of sin because it is God Who created them with that inclination from the very beginning. In a text that resonates for the Christian doctrine of Original Sin, the psalmist declares, "Indeed I was born with iniquity; with sin my mother conceived me." (Psalm 51:7) Surely if we accept the idea that it was God Who created us with this evil inclination, then we can expect that God will be merciful and understanding when we act sinfully as a result of that inclination.

In the rabbinic formulation, the Israelites plead before God, arguing for their innocence, even in the incident of the Golden Calf, because God implanted the evil inclination in them. The people are depicted as claiming no responsibility for the act of idolatry because it was God who implanted in them the evil inclination that led directly to the sinful act. The rabbis want to argue that the Israelites would only want to do God's will were it not for the evil inclination and there is the irony that God created them with the apparent imperfection that itself prevents them from being more obedient. As we will see, and as the rabbis well know, God did not simply leave the Israelites unarmed, without the tools to combat the evil inclination implanted within their character. As usual, the rabbis raise a question for which they already have the answer. Are they responsible for sin given that God implanted the evil inclination that leads them to sin? The rabbis answer in the affirmative because God also gave them the tools, Torah and laws, which they are obligated to use to resist the pull of the evil inclination.

Not only is the evil inclination essential to humans as God created them, it is a part of the human character from birth and God implanted it purposefully. In a Midrash text referring to the Torah verse we noted above, Genesis 8:21, the sages debate the exact moment of the implanting of the evil inclination in humans:

> "For the imagination of man's heart
> is evil from his youth," (Gen. 8:21).
> Rabbi Hiyya the Elder said, "How
> wretched must be the dough when the
> baker himself testifies it to be poor.
> Abba Yose the potter said, "How poor
> must be the leaven when he who
> kneaded it testifies that it is bad." ...
> Antoninus asked Rabbi: "When is
> the evil inclination placed in man?"
> "As soon as he is formed," he replied.

"If so," he objected, "he would dig
through the womb and emerge, rather
it is when he emerges." Rabbi agreed
with him.[7]

Given the choice of the implanting of the evil inclination at the time of the formation of the embryo in the womb or at birth, the rabbis conclude that it happens at birth. Their fundamental conclusion is that the inclination to sin is with a person from the beginning, that there is no period of innocence for an infant or child. With this text they are announcing the conclusion that the evil inclination is a part of the human constitution, that the tendency to sin is not something one acquires from one's environment or from life experience.

In the formulation of the rabbis, the parallel to the evil inclination is the presence of a good inclination, the necessary counter-force to the evil. It is as if we all possess two voices in our spirit, contending with each other as they try to compel the individual to be good or bad. Where the rabbis propose that the evil inclination is present in our character from birth, they argue that we only acquire the good inclination at the age of thirteen years.[8] Jewish tradition holds, in the rabbinic belief, that at the age of thirteen a person is obligated to do the *mitzvot*, or commandments, commanded by God. It is from this tradition that Judaism derives the celebration of becoming *bar mitzvah*, a son of the commandment, at the age of thirteen.[9] Before that age, one's parents are responsible for one's fulfillment of the commandments.

Since the evil inclination is present from birth and the good inclination only emerges at the age of thirteen, the former is older and stronger than the latter. The evil inclination has an age and strength advantage over the good inclination, making the struggle between the two that much more difficult. It is as if the cards are stacked against us in our desire to be good and we need as much help as possible to combat the inclination to sin.

Even in old age a person has to contend with the force of the evil inclination as it continues to lead one to temptation. The struggle with the temptation to sin is never over:

> This one (the evil inclination) grows
> with man from his youth until old
> age, and yet if he can, he strikes him
> down even in his seventies or in his
> eighties.[10]

This battle against the force of the evil inclination is one a person has to fight from birth to death as we contend with an adversary that never relents. This view expressed by the rabbis in Talmud and Midrash teaches that we live our lives from beginning to end with an inclination to sin implanted within us by God. The rabbis never suggest that we can rid ourselves of the evil inclination or live normal lives without the struggle between the two inclinations. It is a lifelong battle ordained by God. The evil inclination turns the heart to evil and leads all people to sin.

Not only is the evil inclination with man from birth to the end of life, but it grows stronger over time. We cannot expect that it will weaken during our lifetime or that we will necessarily become better equipped to defeat or constrain it. In fact, as we become weaker in old age, the evil inclination only becomes stronger. Rabbi Assi, citing Isaiah's (Isaiah 5:18) analogy between sin and a cart rope holds that sin "at first is like a spider's thread, but eventually like a cart rope."[11] We are faced with the daunting challenge of resisting the pull of the evil inclination throughout our lives, a task compounded by the idea that as we age the strength of the inclination only becomes greater and its sting more severe.

In a similar sentiment we read of the increasing strength and power of the evil inclination during a person's lifetime and how it becomes more difficult to combat it:

"Sin couches at the door," (Genesis
2:5)…at first sin is weak, like a
woman, but then it grows strong, like
a man. Rabbi Akiba said, "At first it
is like a spider's web, but eventually
it becomes like a ship's rope…Rabbi
Isaac said, "At first it is like a visitor,
then like a guest and finally like the
master of the house.[12]

People might wonder if there is any relief from the evil inclination
given this rabbinic view that it is implanted by God and present in
us from birth to death. The rabbis pose that question and answer it
with their belief in a world to come, the *olam haba*. The rabbis argue
that there are two worlds, this one in which we live and a world to
come after death. The *olam haba* is the counter-point to this world,
the way in which the apparent injustices and inequities of this world
are reconciled. Righteous people are rewarded in the world to come
and sinners are punished by not achieving or experiencing it. The
messiah will come during the world to come, when final judgment is
executed.

The world to come is also when the evil inclination will finally
be uprooted from the human spirit. In the world to come people will
be liberated from the struggle with the evil inclination and there will
be no need to manage or control it. In fact, throughout the rabbinic
literature, the only use of the word "uproot," (*oker*) is in reference to
the evil inclination; it is the only thing God will uproot from man's
spirit and only in the world to come:

God then said: "in this world they
made idols because of the evil
inclination in them, but in the world

to come I will uproot from them the
evil inclination and give them a heart
of flesh.[13]

Similarly in the passage cited above in which the Israelites plead to
God that they are the imperfect pot made by the potter who left a stone
of evil in the clay, God answers their plea to have the flaw removed,
"This I will do in the time to come."[14] This idea that the evil inclination
will be removed from the human spirit only in the world to come is
repeated in a powerful passage touching on the travails one might have
with life generally and specifically in raising children:

> While in this world, one produces a
> son, brings him to the school, works
> with him, and teaches him Torah.
> Then in the midst of troubles he dies.
> So he derives no happiness from him.
> The Holy One of Blessing said to
> Israel, "In this world, because the evil
> inclination is found in you, you sin
> and your children die. In the world
> to come I will remove the inclination
> from among you. Then you shall have
> children and be happy.[15]

The same idea is expressed in other rabbinic texts:

> The Holy One said, "In this world,
> because the evil inclination exists,
> afflictions exist among the children of
> Adam. But in the world to come I am
> uprooting them out from you.[16]

> The Holy One of Israel: "In this world
> you are anxious over sins, but in the
> world to come, in which there is no

> evil inclination, you will be anxious
> over the good that I have ordained for
> you.[17]

> A definite period was set for the world
> to spend in darkness…for as long as
> the evil inclination exists in the world,
> thick darkness and the shadow of
> death are in the world. When the evil
> inclination will be uprooted from the
> world, thick darkness and the shadow
> of death will pass away from the
> world.[18]

Clearly if the evil inclination will only be uprooted from man's spirit in the world to come then it must be seen as a given and permanent part of the character of man in this world. With the reference above to the presence of the inclination in Adam's children and the texts in which we see that the evil inclination is implanted by the time of birth, we understand that the presence and power of the inclination is universal and lifelong. It was implanted by God as a fixed and essential component of human character and one we must contend with throughout our lives.

1. Throughout this section, any reference to "the rabbis" connotes the rabbis of Talmud and Midrash, the sages whose writings and pronouncements are recorded in those volumes.

2. The world to come, in Hebrew, *olam haba*, is a reflection of the rabbinic view that there are two worlds, this one and the one to come. We live in this world and after death, if our deeds in this one warrant it, we will exist in the world to come. It is the eternal reward for those whose behavior justifies achieving it.

3. Midrash, Genesis Rabbah 27.4

4. Midrash, Genesis Rabbah 9.7

5. Talmud, Berachot 54a

6. Midrash, Exodus Rabbah 46.4

7. Midrash Genesis Rabbah 34.10

8. Midrash Ecclesiastes Rabbah 4.13.1

9. Much later, in the early twentieth century, the tradition of girls reaching the age of religious maturity develops and we have the custom of *bat mitzvah*.

10. Genesis Rabbah 54.1

11. Talmud, Sanhedrin 99b

12. Midrash, Genesis Rabbah 22.6

13. Talmud, Berachot 17a

14. Midrash, Exodus Rabbah 41.7. In the rabbinic usage, the phrase "time to come," (*atid lavo*) is the equivalent to the world to come.

15. Midrash Tanhuma Leviticus 7.14

16. ibid., Genesis 1.40

17. ibid., 3.19

18. Midrash Leviticus Rabbah 89.1

CHAPTER 3 THE MANIFESTATION OF THE EVIL INCLINATION IN RABBINIC LITERATURE

The evil inclination is a powerful and pervasive force within the human spirit. The rabbis believe people have a burden and obligation to combat it throughout their lives. This force draws people to behave badly, to defy God's wishes and is a nearly constant tempter to humans to engage in sin. The particular qualities of the evil inclination and the behavior it compels are of great interest to the rabbis. They describe, at times in vivid detail, the kinds of behavior that are the result of the presence of this persistent force in the human character. While the rabbis are not themselves systematic in cataloging the behaviors, in reviewing the relevant texts they can be organized into three categories: sexual relations, aggression and violence, and idolatrous rebellion against God.

In a general statement about the kind of behavior to which the evil inclination will lead people, the rabbis observe that it will lead us precisely to acts that are forbidden:

> The *yetzer hara* craves only what
> is forbidden. This is illustrated in
> the following: Rabbi Mana went
> up to visit Rabbi Haggai [on Yom
> Kippur, the Day of Atonement, a
> day of fasting]; Haggai was feeling
> weak. Mana said to him, "Go drink
> something." He left him and went
> away. After a while he came back
> to him. He said to him, "What
> happened to your thirst?" He said to
> him, "When you gave me permission
> [to drink], it went away. [1]

As we commonly experience with children, the forbidden becomes the desired. It is, according to the rabbis, in the very nature of the human personality to desire that which has been prohibited. The rabbis are telling us that the evil inclination, in its simplest form, is the fundamental expression of the human desire for the forbidden. The evil inclination leads people directly to violate God's rules about that which cannot be done, to engage in sin. In the case cited here, as soon as the rabbi is permitted to commit an act that is otherwise prohibited, i.e. drink on Yom Kippur, he no longer wants to do it. The evil inclination had driven him to want something to drink on Yom Kippur and his desire was not so much for the water as it was to violate the law.

The evil inclination is frequently associated with the vigor, energy and the excesses of youth, with the unrestrained exuberance of youthfulness. During adolescence the battle between the force and strength of the evil and good inclinations is joined. The rabbis recognize that young people are inclined to acts of excess and see this as the result of the evil inclination's influence. They also hold that one needs to grow and mature and learn the limits and boundaries that come from the presence of the good inclination. Rabbinic Judaism does not call for or expect asceticism or complete self-denial but calls upon people to be aware that the evil inclination will lead to rejoicing and possible excess. While understanding that especially in one's youth one may succumb to the force of the evil inclination, the rabbis at the same time expect the person to exercise the limiting controls of the good inclination. It is a difficult and challenging balancing act, which the rabbis fully understood, and it is made all the more difficult by the allure of the sinful acts associated with the evil inclination and the relative immaturity and weakness of the good inclination.

Young men and women are likely to give in to the temptations of sin, and it is that very surrender that led, according to the rabbis, to the ultimate disaster, the destruction of the Temple in Jerusalem. One rabbi held that the Temple was destroyed precisely because of the misbehavior of young people:

> They (the young women) would take
> myrrh and balsam and place it in
> their shoes and when they came near
> the young men of Israel they would
> kick, causing the balsam to squirt at
> them and would thus cause the evil
> inclination to enter them (the young
> men) like an adder's poison.[2]

In rabbinic thought, sexual desire lies at the root of the power of the evil inclination, starting in one's youth and continuing throughout one's lifetime. Men are enticed by women, in the rabbinic formulation, and the allure and enticement of women is the work of the evil inclination. It is this very allure that must be fought off with the force of the good inclination. The rabbis express their concerns about anyone who might leave himself vulnerable to the power of sexual desire brought on by the evil inclination:

> Rabbi Giddal was accustomed to go
> and sit at the gates of the ritual bath.
> He used to say to the women, "Bathe
> this way," or, "Bathe this way." The
> rabbis said to him, "Is not the master
> afraid lest his desires get the better of
> him?" He replied, "They look to me
> like so many white geese."[3]

The "white geese" are creatures that are objectively attractive and appealing, but to Rabbi Giddal, the women are no more objects of desire than these animals. It is the other rabbis who expressed their concern that he might be tempting his evil inclination by sitting outside the bath and speaking to the women.

The rabbis held that whenever men and women are together there is the possibility, if not the likelihood, of sexual attraction. That sexual attraction and the tendency to act on it are results of the power and force of the evil inclination. In the midst of a discussion about when it is permissible for men and women to be together, the question is raised about their presence at a cemetery. A disagreement between two sages is highlighted by a declarative statement that men and women can be together because, "Sexual desire is not common in a graveyard."[4] The same concern regarding the presence of men and women together and the potential for arousal of sexual desire is raised in the context of the world to come. The sages wonder whether in *olam haba*, the world to come, when the evil inclination has no power, if men and women can be together. The clear implication is that in our times, in this world, when the evil inclination does have power over people, men and women cannot be together because the evil inclination will lead them to illicit sexual desire or behavior.

Sexual desire is, in the rabbinic view, not always a bad thing, and in fact in many cases is regarded as good and necessary, as we saw in the midrash text regarding the necessity of the evil inclination. In the biblical book of Ruth, Ruth is a Moabite woman who had been married to an Israelite man. When he dies, leaving her widowed, she is encouraged to remain in her ancestral home and instead commits to staying with her mother-in-law and to journey with her back to the Land of Israel. There Ruth harvests grain from the field of a man, Boaz, who turns out to be a distant relative. In the story the question arises as to who will redeem Ruth as a widowed relative and marry her, according to Biblical law and custom. The rabbis, in commenting on the text, identify Boaz' admirable willingness to fulfill the commitment of the redeeming kinsman as an expression of his evil inclination:

> Rabbi Judah bar Rabbi Shallum the Levite said, "The *yetzer hara* came to him (Boaz). It said to him, "You are unmarried. Take her." Immediately he bound his inclination by an oath and said to it, "As Adonai lives," (Ruth 3:13) I will not touch her.[5]

In this brief passage we see a reflection of the intense and complex struggle that the rabbis believe is the hallmark of all good people. Boaz, like any decent person, struggles with his good and evil inclination. The voice of the evil inclination tells him he is single and can have sex with Ruth. He then "bound his inclination" with his good voice, which told him not to touch her. He goes on to fulfill the commandment to redeem her as a widowed kinsman, but controls his sexual urges so that the sexual desire is not presumably the primary force moving him to act. For Boaz and virtually all of us, life is a struggle between the urges of the two inclinations and the evil inclination may move us to do things that are necessary and even ultimately good, but it must be controlled, managed, "bound up" by the good inclination.

The evil inclination can even tempt a sage to ponder acts of sexual impropriety; the rabbis tell us that every man can be enticed by a woman at least to give thought to violating sexual prohibitions. The very consideration of such actions is deemed a sin and the effect of the ever-present evil inclination:

> Every time Rabbi Hiyya bar Abba fell
> upon his face (in prayer) he used to
> say, "The Merciful save us from the
> evil inclination." One day his wife
> heard him. "Let us see," she thought,
> "as it is so many years that he has held
> himself away from me, why should
> he be praying these words?" One day,
> while he was studying in his garden,
> she adorned herself (so he could not
> recognize her) and repeatedly walked
> up and down before him. "Who are
> you" he demanded. "I am Haruta, and
> have returned today," she replied. He
> desired her. She said to him, "Bring
> me that pomegranate from the highest
> branch." He jumped up, went, and
> brought it to her. When he came
> back to his house, his wife was firing
> the oven and he went in and sat in
> it. "What does this mean?" she asked
> him. He told her what had happened.
> "It was I," she assured him, but he
> paid no heed to her until she gave him
> proof. "Nevertheless," he said, "my
> intent was evil."[6]

In this intriguing story, Rabbi Hiyya has apparently declined to engage in sexual relations with his wife for a considerable period of time, itself an odd form of virtue in rabbinic tradition. Sexual relations between husband and wife are expected, even required as a part of the marital relationship, and in fact, in other rabbinic texts, refusal of conjugal relations is justification for divorce. Rabbi Hiyya has committed to a celibate life and prays to avoid even thinking about sex and is troubled by the fact that he is feeling lustful toward his disguised wife. When she tries to reassure him since he did not in fact try to have sex with what he thought was another woman, he declares that the very thought about having sex is a sin resulting from his evil inclination. The Talmud text goes on to say that Hiyya fasted the rest of his life after this incident, until he died. He is referred to as a righteous person in the account of his fasting and dying. His wife seemed content, having proven to herself that he still needed to pray to resist his evil inclination, but he believed himself a failure for not having successfully controlled the inclination after a prolonged period of prayer and abstinence. From this text we learn that sexual desire is an expression of the evil inclination and that it is a powerful force, even for a sage committed to a life of prayer and abstinence.

The inclination compels a person to desire women sexually, but one always has the obligation, ability and opportunity to resist the pull and the temptations of the desire. To resist the strength of the evil inclination is a virtue, a level achieved only by the most righteous:

> We (two anonymous men) went in
> two together to each woman and
> one of us would blacken her face
> and the other take off her ornaments
> (apparently two ways to make the
> woman less appealing). Is it possible
> that our desire was not excited ever
> so little? On account of that slight
> excess of desire we propose to bring
> an offering….For everyone who has
> the opportunity of committing a sin
> and escapes it and refrains from doing
> it performs a highly religious act….
> Everyone who stands up against his
> *yetzer hara* and masters it is called a

> mighty man as for the instance Moses
> in his day, David in his day, Ezra in his
> day.[7]

The reference to David is especially odd given his sexual encounter with Bat Sheva and subsequent designation of her husband, Uriah, David's long-time trusted general, to death in battle. Surely David can be seen as a prime example of a person who, while otherwise expressing devotion to God, in at least one instance submitted to his evil inclination. David is a "mighty man," but he is also a man who allowed his evil inclination to run amok in this one famous incident.

The evil inclination leads men to sexual desire and to consider, if not act upon, illicit sexual acts. The ideal form of behavior is to engage in sexual activity only in limited circumstances, certainly only in the context of marriage and even then, apparently not to excess. Any other sexual activity is seen as a rebellion against God and is matched in rabbinic thought by the evil inclination's power to drive men to the ultimate form of rebellion against God, idolatry. Worshipping idols is, of course, never permissible, even under pain of death, and so it constitutes a total rejection of God. Illicit sexual behavior is only a rejection of God's commandments, but still is regarded as a rebellion against God's dominion over our lives. The rabbis also recognize that it is far easier for people to avoid idolatry than to resist the pull of sexual activity, that we can realistically expect to defeat the one but can only hope to manage and direct sexual desires:

> Rabbi Hunia said in the name of
> Rabbi Dosa ben Tevet, "God created
> two evil inclinations in His world,
> the inclination to idolatry and the
> inclination to sexual behavior. The
> inclination to idolatry has already been
> uprooted. The inclination to sexual
> behavior still exists. Says the Holy

> One of Blessing, "If one can resist the
> inclination to sexual activity, I account
> it to him as if he had withstood
> both."[8]

It is characteristic of rabbinic literature that a view expressed in one text does not agree with the view expressed on the same subject somewhere else. In this case, while the text quoted above states that God has uprooted idolatry from the human inclination to sin, in another text, sexual misbehavior can itself lead a person to engage in idolatry:

> Rab stated: "A man who willfully
> brings about an erection should be
> placed under a ban." But why didn't
> he say, "This is forbidden." Because the
> man has provoked the *yetzer hara* only
> against himself. Rabbi Ammi however
> stated, "He is called a rebel, because
> such is the act of the *yetzer hara*. Today
> it provokes a man to do one wrong
> thing, and tomorrow it incites him
> to worship idols and he goes on to
> worship them."[9]

The idea that the strategy of the evil inclination is to entice a person to commit one sin one day and the worse sin of idolatry the next day is conveyed in this passage discussing expressions of anger and providing some insight into the rabbis' view of sinful behavior:

> He who tears his garments in his
> anger, he who breaks his vessels in his
> anger, and he who scatters his money
> in his anger, regard him as an idolater,
> because such are the ways of the *yetzer*

> *hara*—today he says to him, "Do this,"
> and tomorrow he tells him, "Do that,"
> until it (the *yetzer hara)* entices him,
> "Go and serve idols," and he goes and
> serves them. [10]

We would note that here the evil inclination is associated with lack of control over one's emotions, especially anger. Apparently this lack of anger management can unleash a general lack of control that can then lead to committing acts of idolatry. The associations of the evil inclination with idolatry suggest that the rabbis identify it with the greatest of violations of God's will and with the very denial of God. Lesser violations, like the expression of rage and sexual behavior, while sinful and the results of the evil inclination, can be gateways to this ultimate transgression.

As the ultimate act of rejection of God, idolatry confounds and disturbs the rabbis and they have to find some explanation for how any Jew could engage in the behavior. Something powerful must be present to compel a Jew to engage in such an act or even a consideration of it. In one instance they hold that wine, like the evil inclination, can confuse people enough that it will lead them to worship an idol:

> Rabbi Meir said, "The community of
> Israel said, 'The *yetzer hara* obtained
> mastery over me like wine, and I said
> to the (golden) calf, 'This is your god,
> O Israel.'" (Exodus 32:4) When wine
> goes into a man it confuses his mind.[11]

In several places the sins associated with the evil inclination are acts of aggression, violence and murder. Cain in Genesis is associated with the ultimate act of aggression and violence and with the evil inclination:

> There are three strong desires. The
> yearning of Israel is only toward their
> father in heaven…The longing of a
> woman is only for her husband…The
> longing of the *yetzer hara* is for Cain
> and his like.[12]

This association between the evil inclination and violent behavior is explicitly stated, and the only hope for relief, as we have already seen, is in the world to come:

> God said, "In this world, because the
> *yetzer hara* is present, men kill one
> another and die, but in the time to
> come I will uproot the *yetzer hara*
> from your midst and there will be no
> death in the world.[13]

While not nearly so heinous as sexual misbehavior, idolatry or aggression and violence, gluttony is another area of behavior that the rabbis associate with the evil inclination:

> Now the *yetzer hara* says, "Let us eat,
> drink and fulfill all our desires," but
> the good inclination says, "Let us
> not eat and drink, but be occupied
> with Torah." Then we heed the
> *yetzer hara*. Why? Because it is bigger
> than all of them…no one heeds
> the good inclination, because it is
> insignificant.[14]

All of these behaviors are understood as rejections of the kind of behavior desired by God. We have this irony then, in which God implanted this evil inclination that is with us for a lifetime, is powerful and forceful, and which leads us directly to engage in behavior God rejects. God gave us the good inclination as well, but it is weaker, less powerful than the evil inclination. The imbalance can only be rectified by reliance on God and God's laws. Life in this world is distinguished by the push and pull as people are drawn by a good inclination to obey God's commandments but are pulled away by this more established and stronger evil inclination. Surely there is some reason God has presented us with this struggle and there must a way for us to understand and engage in, even be victorious in the struggle.

1. Palestinian Talmud, Yoma 6.43d

2. Talmud, Yoma 9b

3. Talmud, Berachot 20a

4. Palestinian Talmud, Kiddushin 4.66b

5. Palestinian Talmud, Sukkot 5.55b

6. Talmud, Kiddushin 81b

7. Midrash, Song of Songs Rabbah 4.4.3

8. ibid., 7.8.1

9. Talmud, Niddah 13b

10. Talmud, Shabbat 105b

11. Midrash Song of Songs Rabbah 2.4.1

12. ibid., 7.11.1

13. Midrash, Deuteronomy Rabbah 2.30

14. Midrash, Tanhuma Genesis 11.1

CHAPTER 4   THE STRUGGLE WITH THE EVIL INCLINATION IN RABBINIC LITERATURE

The rabbis hold that everyone has to struggle between the strength and power of the two inclinations, the evil and the good. They believe it is a difficult struggle between strong and durable forces, a struggle in which we can have temporary but no permanent success. This teaching of the rabbis states that it is in the choosing between the good and evil inclinations that humans establish what it is to be human. People are defined by the fact that they make this choice and that it is a difficult and demanding choice, since there is always the temptation to follow the evil inclination. In a cryptic passage in Ecclesiastes, we read, "There was a little city, with few men in it; and to it came a great king, who invested it and built mighty siege works against it. Present in the city was a poor wise man who might have saved it with his wisdom, but nobody thought of that poor man." (Ecclesiastes 9:14) The cryptic nature of the passage leaves a great opening for rabbis to bring to bear their interpretive powers and they understand the verse to be a tale of metaphor and allegory:

> "Now there was a little city," that is
> the body, "And few men within it,"
> that is the limbs. "And there came a
> great king against it," the *yetzer hara*.
> Why is it called "great"? Because it
> is thirteen years older than the *yetzer
> hatov*. "Now there was found in it a
> man poor and wise," that is the *yetzer
> hatov*. Why is it called "poor"? Because
> it is not found in all persons, nor do
> most of them obey it.[1]

In identifying these elements of the verse as metaphors in a larger allegory of a city besieged by a powerful king with a poor wise man in it, the rabbis teach that the two inclinations are in a struggle with each other. It is, they suggest, like a war with a siege led by a mighty king, the evil inclination, and it is opposed by a good inclination that is poor and weak. The good inclination could save the city, the person, except for its weakness and the fact that people do not listen to it. These vivid images tell us, in the interpretation of the rabbis, that these two contending forces are battling for control of the individual. The evil inclination must be powerful because it draws men away from obedience to God's commandments. They view the evil inclination as exercising a ruling or dominating force over the affairs of men and so associate it with a king.

The rabbis depict the evil inclination as a dynamic force that grows and strengthens over the years. These battling forces of the two inclinations fight for the control of each person's behavior and his or her performance of the commandments:

It often happens that when one is
eager to fulfill a commandment his
yetzer hara within him dissuades him,
saying, "Why do you want to perform
this commandment and decrease your
wealth? Instead of giving it away to
others, give it to your own children."
But the *yetzer hatov* says to him, "Give
rather to a pious cause."[2]

In the battle to control the evil inclination the rabbis often use the
language of governing and ruling, suggesting that people have to find
ways to have the good inclination rule over or dominate the evil. This
language of rulership seems to express the idea that the evil inclination
is undisciplined, even chaotic and powerful, and that in the struggle
with the good inclination it cannot be vanquished, but can only be
controlled, managed, or dominated. This idea of ruling over the evil
inclination is central to the Jewish conception of these contending
forces or inclinations. People cannot expect to eliminate or destroy the
evil inclination and it will, as we have seen, only be finally uprooted
in the world to come, after death. The realistic and attainable goal in
this view is to use the good inclination to corral and manage the evil
inclination. This struggle to rule over the evil inclination is one that
cannot be waged alone and one which will not be won easily if at all:

Rabbah ben Bar Hana said, "The
prophet urged Israel, 'Return and
repent.' They replied, 'We cannot:
the *yetzer hara* rules over us.' He said
to them, 'Curb your desires.' They
replied, 'Let God, who is master over
the *yetzer hara* teach us to curb our
desires."[3]

The sage is teaching that only with God's help can the people control and rule over the urges of the evil inclination, that we need God to teach us how to do it. It is never suggested that God will destroy the inclination so that people do not have to contend with it any more.

In the midrash passage to Ecclesiastes 9:14 that is cited above the rabbis offered the interpretation of the great king of the city as the evil inclination and the poor wise man as the good inclination. There is the irony in this interpretation that the poor wise man has to find a way to rule over and dominate the great king. The rabbis are indicating how very difficult it is to control the urges of the evil inclination, how the situation is not set up in favor of the person struggling to dominate the evil inclination. It takes great strength, even the strength of a monarch, to rule over a force as powerful and dominating as a king:

> Another interpretation (of the king
> in Proverbs 24:21, "Fear the Lord,
> my son, and the king…"): Be king
> over the *yetzer hara*, which is called a
> king (referencing the Ecclesiastes 9:14
> text).[4]

The rabbis offer this recurring imagery of the evil inclination as a ruler and the need for the corresponding force of a strong sovereign to combat it. This idea is expressed explicitly regarding the two inclinations doing battle within the human spirit:

> Another interpretation is that the
> words, "he ruled" (from Proverbs
> 24:21) means, "Make your *yetzer hatov*
> ruler over your *yetzer hara* which is
> termed "king."[5]

A similar point about ruling over the evil inclination is made in a discussion about adultery, where the language of reigning in the context of the evil inclination is used:

> Raba declared, "We have learned a
> tradition that the *yetzer hara* only rules
> over what a person's eye can see."[6]

This would suggest that if a person avoids looking at temptation, whether it be the possibility of engaging in a sexual relationship or contemplating assaulting a person physically, one can avoid the pull and force of the evil inclination. One way to avoid succumbing to the evil inclination is to avoid the ordinary temptations of life. It is so difficult, according to this view, to rule over and control the evil inclination that the more effective strategy is to avoid any visual engagement or temptation.

The righteous people in a community are distinguished not by the absence of an evil inclination but by this very ability to rule over it. There are singular righteous people, like some of the leading figures in the Bible, but in most cases even they are depicted as only ruling over their inclination:

> "All the armor of the warriors." This
> includes in addition all who stand and
> rule over their *yetzer hara* and master
> it, like Moses in his day, David in his
> day, Ezra in his day. The whole of the
> generation of such a man depends on
> him.[7]

Once again we would note that the inclusion of David in this passage is curious, given his actions regarding Bat Sheva and the plot to have her husband, Uriah, killed in battle so the king could have his way with her. The rabbis deal with the patriarch Abraham and King David in different ways, and in doing so, declare that ordinary people cannot expect to be included in this rarefied atmosphere:

> Abraham our forefather even
> transformed the *yetzer hara* into good.
> Said Rabbi Aha, "He made a deal
> (with his evil desire) so that he could
> control it." But David could not
> withstand the power of the evil desire
> and he had to destroy it.[8]

David is the only person mentioned in the rabbinic literature who manages to destroy his evil inclination. That would appear to stem from the dilemma facing the rabbis regarding David. On one hand they regard the great monarch as righteous and on the other they have to acknowledge that his behavior, especially as regards his lust for and sexual relationship with Bat Sheva and his conspiracy against her husband, Uriah, (II Samuel 11) was not virtuous. In the episode with Bat Sheva, he sees a beautiful woman, has her brought to him and while knowing she was married, has sex with her. Not only was she married, she was married to an officer who had been loyal to David for years. He then proceeds to have her husband, Uriah, killed in battle. In this sordid episode he would certainly appear to be acting on the desires of his evil inclination. The rabbis' problem is not only that David is a great Israelite king, but he is the father of the next great Israelite king, Solomon, and in the rabbinic tradition David is the progenitor of the messiah. Their solution for this conundrum was to conclude that he singularly finds a way to destroy his evil inclination, an inclination that seemed to be especially strong in his spirit. They do not bother to explain how he managed to destroy his evil inclination.

David may have destroyed his evil inclination, but only two other Biblical figures, along with David, successfully ruled over their evil inclination. The three used oaths to achieve this lofty goal. Each of the three, in their Biblical stories, was faced with situations of sexual desire and temptation:

> Rabbi Yose said, "There were three
> whose passions threatened to
> overpower them and who checked
> them with a pledge, i.e. Joseph, David
> and Boaz.[9]

The passage goes on to cite their temptation to act out sexually and their pledges not to follow the inclination's allure. In no case are these tempted and righteous figures seen as above temptation, but rather able to use their strength of character, their good inclination, to resist the sexual desires that every person has. Ruling over one's evil inclination is no small matter and requires, even from the righteous of the Bible, willpower, an oath and the full strength one can muster. A person distinguishes himself as righteous not with the absence of evil inclination, but with mastery over it.

The rabbis characterize Joseph as righteous, despite his seemingly insensitive behavior toward his family in the depiction and sharing of his dreams (Genesis 37). Joseph manifests his virtuous character clearly in the episode with Potiphar's wife (Genesis 39), in which she tries to seduce him and fails. He is one of these figures who can be tempted to act on his evil inclination but has the strength to follow the good inclination and resist temptation.

The patriarchs of the Bible, Abraham, Isaac, and Jacob, are among the very few, according to the rabbis, who are not subject to the pull and influence of the evil inclination. Their distinctively righteous nature seems to make them immune to the pull of the inclination and so they do not face the struggle all other people do. With them, the evil inclination has no control or power:

> There were three over whom the
> *yetzer hara* had no dominion, that is
> Abraham, Isaac and Jacob...Some
> include David.[10]

The wicked, by definition, are those who succumb to the evil inclination, giving in to its enticements without a struggle. In the rabbinic view, this is the distinguishing feature that sets apart the wicked from the righteous. It is not that the righteous do not have an evil inclination and the wicked do, but that the former manage to control and rule over theirs and the wicked succumb to its urges. The Genesis figure, Esau, older twin brother of Jacob, son of Isaac and Rebeccah, is regarded in rabbinic literature as the prime example of a wicked person and is described as giving in to his evil inclination:

> "And Esau hated Jacob." (Genesis 27:41) Rabbi Leazar ben Rabbi Yose said, "He was filled with hatred, hostility, and vindictiveness toward him (Jacob),....The wicked stand in subjection to their heart....But the righteous have their hearts under their control."[11]

What makes a person righteous is the ability to make conscious and deliberate decisions to exercise control over the evil inclination and to allow the good inclination to rule over their lives. The wicked are those who allow free rein to their evil inclination, making no or too little effort to control its urges. Each person is confronted by a fundamental choice throughout his or her life and the decisions a person makes determines the moral character of the individual:

> He who chooses the *yetzer hatov* in preference to the *yetzer hara* would be the righteous. And the one who chooses the *yetzer hara* in preference to the *yetzer hatov* would be the wicked.[12]

The enduring struggle between the evil and good inclinations is waged on several fronts and can be fought with various strategies. It is a struggle that can be won in the moment, as depicted in a tale of the approaching Sabbath and the conflict between the commandment to observe the sacred day and the obligation of aiding a person in need:

> Abba Tachna the Pious was entering his city on the eve of the Sabbath at dusk with his bundle thrown over his shoulder, when he met a man afflicted with boils lying at the junction. The man said to him, "Rabbi, do me an act of righteousness and carry me into the city." He (Abba) remarked, "If I abandon my bundle, from where shall I and my household support ourselves? But if I abandon this sick man I will give up my life." What did he do? He allowed the *yetzer hatov* to master the *yetzer hara* and carried the afflicted man into the city. He then returned for his bundle and entered at sunset. Everyone was amazed (that he was violating the Sabbath rules by carrying something into the city) and said, "Is this Abba Tachna the Pious?" He felt uneasy in his heart and said, "Do you think that I perhaps desecrated the Sabbath?" At that time the Holy One of Blessing caused the sun to shine.[13]

Abba Tachna struggled between his two inclinations in this ironic passage, the good one telling him to help the sick man, the evil one telling him to follow the laws of Shabbat and disregard the person in need. The irony rests in the rabbinic idea expressed here that the evil inclination would be telling someone to adhere to the Sabbath laws. Surely the rabbis did not believe that Sabbath observance was sinful or evil, but rather that in choosing between compassion for a sick person and adherence to ritual laws, that compassion must win out. They go so far as to suggest that in the conflict between the two, siding with obedience to the laws over performing an act of compassion is the choice of the evil inclination. They teach that compassion is what God wants us to choose, the choice of the good inclination, as evidenced by the statement that the sun shone later than it should have so that Abba would not be violating the Sabbath after all. God, according to the rabbis, will reverse the course of the universe to support compassion over law, the good inclination over the evil.

A strange and intense tale is told in the rabbinic literature of an otherwise obscure rabbi who is tempted by Satan in a manner similar to Job in the Bible. God attests to his righteousness and Satan asks to test him and unlike with Job, this sage, Rabbi Matthew ben Heresh, is tempted by a desirable woman, touching on the recurring theme of the rabbis that sexual desire lies at the core of the evil inclination. Rabbi Matthew ben Heresh resists the temptation by averting his gaze from the woman and Satan keeps trying to encourage him to succumb to lust. The sage goes so far as to ask his students to blind him with fiery hot needles in his eyes. As a consequence of this struggle, as personified by the contest between God and Satan, God is depicted as saying to the heroic and virtuous rabbi:

> "From this day on do not fear. I am
> standing surety for you in this matter,
> that the *yetzer hara* will never prevail
> against you all the days of your life"....
> Here is the origin of what the sages
> have said, "Whoever does not look
> at another woman will not have the
> *yetzer hara* prevailing against him."[14]

Despite their best efforts people will, at various times in their lives, stumble over the evil inclination. It is a constant obstacle facing people in their daily lives and one that can bring a person to evil at any unsuspecting moment:

> "For you have stumbled over that which leads you to evil." (Hosea 14:2) Rabbi Simon compared the *yetzer hara* with a stone sticking up at a crossroads, a stone which men were always stumbling over. The king of the region said, "Keep chipping away at the stone until the time comes for me to have it removed entirely from its place. So, too the Holy One said to Israel, "My children, the *yetzer hara* is the outstanding cause of the world's stumbling. Keep chipping away at it until the time comes for Me to have it removed entirely from the hearts of man.[15]

Even a priest of the sacrificial system of the Temple can, according to the rabbis, be drawn to sexual activity by his evil inclination. In a discussion of the permissibility of sexually desiring a captive woman, based on a verse in Deuteronomy, ("…and you see among the captives a beautiful woman and you desire her and would take her to wife." Deuteronomy 21:11) the rabbis discuss the nature of desire as it is incited by the evil inclination:

> With respect to the first intercourse (between the priest and the woman) there is universal agreement that it is permitted, since the Torah provided for man's evil desires. The dispute (between two rabbis) refers only to the second intercourse. Rav ruled it

> is permitted and Samuel ruled it is
> forbidden…since the Torah provided
> for man's evil desires.[16]

The question here is whether what the rabbis describe as the Torah's universally accepted and acknowledged provision for acting out on the evil desires can apply to two or only one act of intercourse. Passion is the function of the evil inclination and is accepted as a human reality, but then one has to wonder whether the good inclination should be taking over or not. Apparently even the Torah cannot be expected to keep a person from acting on his evil inclination, but it can be expected to keep people from making it a regular, intentional practice. If even a priest is presumed to have an evil inclination and to act on it, it can be presumed that ordinary people certainly would as well.

The rabbinic view is not so simple as to suggest that there are merely righteous and wicked people in the world and that everyone can be placed into one category or another. They are well aware that all people are able at times to act according to the power of the good inclination and that everyone, at times, succumbs to the desires of the evil inclination. The rabbis recognize that in fact, there are only very few people at either extreme, people who either live almost completely according to the good or evil inclination. They put forth the premise that most people gravitate at one time or another to the good or evil inclinations and that all of us struggle with both inclinations throughout our lives:

> It has been taught: Rabbi Yose the
> Galilean says, "The righteous are
> judged by their *yetzer hatov*…the
> wicked are judged by their *yetzer
> hara*…Average people are swayed by
> both inclinations.[17]

Running throughout the rabbinic discussion of the evil inclination and the struggle to overcome its pull and attraction is the recognition that there are, in their belief, four categories of people in the world. Most are ordinary people who move between resisting and succumbing to the evil inclination, who struggle with it as a lifelong endeavor. They are engaged in a constant battle to dominate and rule over the evil inclination, able to rely on Torah and God's laws to resist its pull, but often inexplicably refusing or failing to do so. The second category is wicked people who routinely succumb to the power of the evil inclination; they are rarely singled out or named by the rabbis. Beyond naming singularly wicked people in the Bible like Esau or Amalek, it seems people are supposed to know who they are. Finally, there are two categories of righteous people that can be called the ordinary and the stellar. The ordinary righteous include sages whom the rabbis identify in various places, rabbis who consistently and regularly are able to resist the temptation. They are depicted as using the force of Torah in their lives to avoid even the greatest of temptations of women who offer themselves for carnal pleasures for the night. The fourth category of people, the stellar righteous, are those found only in the Bible and they are the only people who live without the struggle of the rest of humanity. The stellar righteous mentioned in the rabbinic literature include the patriarchs, Joseph, Moses, King David, Ezra and Boaz.

No women are ever mentioned as possessing an evil inclination and are never referred to in the description of the struggle of men. This presumably is a result of the male-centered nature of the rabbinic culture and texts. Women's desires and urges are never discussed by the rabbis and they are typically objectified as those who incite the passions and desires of men. The rabbis do not understand women to be beings who have to struggle with their own evil inclination, perhaps because they simply do not understand women very well. The rabbinic world was very largely a man's world, with women primarily serving functions, albeit important ones like homemaking and child-rearing.

As we have seen, the struggle with the evil inclination lasts a lifetime and it is one all of us have to wage. No one can know to what extent he will succeed in the struggle in some ultimate sense until the end of life. Even the righteous will only be judged regarding their battle with the inclinations after their death:

> The Holy One of Blessing does not
> call the righteous man holy until he
> is laid away in the earth. Why not?
> Because the *yetzer hara* keeps pressing
> him. And so God does not put His
> trust in him in this world till the day
> of his death....Rabbi Aha bar Papa
> taught, "What is meant by the verse,
> 'He draws away the mighty also by his
> power?' (Job 24:22) It means that the
> *yetzer hara*, by its power, draws even
> the mighty away.[18]

To combat the evil inclination effectively a person has to understand it as fully as possible, seeking to understand its strength, its allure, its power to entice. In understanding it people have a greater possibility of managing and controlling it:

> According to Rabbi Abba, the verse
> (Proverbs 19:17) alludes to him who
> sees to it that his *yetzer hatov* has
> thorough knowledge of his *yetzer
> hara*.[19]

This lifelong struggle between the power of the two inclinations is a demanding one and one that for the vast majority of us will never fully be resolved. It is a struggle that will require great personal strength and tools that God provides if people choose to use them. It is the very struggle, according to this rabbinic view, that defines humanity. People are inclined to sin, to act according to the desires of the evil inclination, not because it is in human character to sin, but because it is in the human character to have to struggle with the two inclinations. The rabbis also put forth the view that God provided the tools to manage the struggle, to be successful as often as possible in the critical goal of ruling over the evil inclination.

1. Midrash Ecclesiastes Rabbah 9.15.8

2. Midrash Exodus Rabbah 16.3

3. Talmud, Sanhedrin 105a

4. Midrash Tanhuma, Numbers 3.16

5. Midrash Numbers Rabbah 15.14

6. Talmud, Sotah 8a

7. Midrash Song of Songs Rabbah 4.4.1

8. Midrash Leviticus Rabbah 23.11

9. Palestinian Talmud, Berachot 9.14b

10. Midrash, Genesis Rabbah 67.8

11. Talmud, Baba Batra 17a

12. Midrash, Ecclesiastes Rabbah 9.2

13. Midrash Ecclesiastes Rabbah 9.7.1

14. Midrash, Tanhuma Genesis 6.1

15. Midrash, Pesikta deRab Kahana 24.17

16. Talmud, Kiddushin 22b

17. Talmud, Berachot 61b

18. Midrash, Psalms Rabbah 16.2

19. Midrash, Psalms Rabbah 41.2

CHAPTER 5   STRATEGIES FOR COMBATING THE EVIL INCLINATION IN RABBINIC LITERATURE

It would be cruel and unmerciful for God to create people with the battling inclinations and then not to provide any tools and devices for waging that battle. What sense could a person make of a God who left people abandoned, only inevitably to succumb to the evil inclination and sin against the divine commands? The rabbis of Talmud and Midrash put forth a vision of a God who implanted the inclinations within humans, knowing people would struggle throughout their lives to follow the urges of the good inclination, and likely to succumb at times to the evil. Their vision included a God Who also provides people with the tools to wage this lifelong and demanding struggle. It is up to each person whether and how successfully to use the tools at his or her disposal, whether to engage the struggle to manage and rule over the evil inclination or to succumb and sin.

People generally do not do enough, according to the rabbis, to control their evil inclination, as one can see from the results in human sinfulness. People use all kinds of tools in their lives to accomplish tasks but ignore the tools God has provided to control the evil inclination. In a discussion of the goads one may use to control a heifer, or cow, the point is made regarding the use of tools to manage the evil inclination:

> A man provides a goad for his heifer,
> but he provides no such goad for his
> *yetzer hara*.[1]

People are not expected to combat and be successful against the evil inclination only with the personal tools of mind and spirit. The rabbis believe people must use tools provided by God to wage this difficult battle.

One of the strategies a person can use to control the evil inclination is prayer. Through prayer a person can summon the strength to resist the enticements of the evil inclination and turn to God for strength in resisting its pull:

> Mar the son of Rabina concluded his
> prayer adding the following: "…Open
> my heart in Your law, and may my
> soul pursue Your commandments, and
> deliver me from evil fortune, from the
> *yetzer hara* and from an evil woman
> and from all evils that threaten to
> come upon the world.[2]

This prayer of a rabbi suggests that one can, through this kind of supplication to God, summon the strength to resist the urges of the evil inclination and to resist the temptations of all forms of evil. Much of Jewish prayer is communal, offered in the plural as the one who prays considers the needs and yearnings of the praying community. Some prayers are offered in the singular and can be intensely personal. One

of these is the recitation of Sh'ma offered at bedtime,[3] which includes
the following expression as recorded in the Talmud:

> May it be Your will, O Lord, my God,
> to make me lie down in peace, and set
> my portion in Your law and accustom
> me to the performance of religious
> duties, but do not accustom me to
> transgression. Bring me not into sin,
> or into iniquity, or into temptation,
> or into contempt. And may the *yetzer*
> *hatov* have sway over me and not let
> the *yetzer hara* control me. And deliver
> me from evil fortune and diseases, and
> let not evil dreams and evil thoughts
> disturb me.[4]

This personal and private prayer, offered in solitude before going
to sleep, expresses the rabbinic view that there are grave dangers in the
world, especially in the dark of night and when one sleeps. Succumbing
to the evil inclination is one of these dangers and this nighttime prayer
offers the hope that God will protect a person from this danger and the
others that surround us.

Prayer is one of the tools suggested by the rabbis in the battle with
the evil inclination and another one cited frequently is the Torah,
specifically the act of studying Torah. The rabbis believe that immersion
in God's words and laws will enable a person to resist the urges of the
inclination. If one strategy does not work, perhaps the other will:

> Rabbi Levi ben Chama says in the
> name of Rabbi Simeon ben Lakish,
> "A man should always incite the *yetzer*
> *hatov* to fight against the *yetzer hara*.
> For it is written, "Tremble and do not
> sin." (Psalms 4:5) If he subdues it,

well and good. If not, let him study
Torah. For it is written, "Commune
with your own heart." (Psalms 4:5)
If he subdues it, well and good. If
not, let him recite the *Sh'ma*. For
it is written, "upon your bed." If he
subdues it, well and good. If not, let
him remind himself on the day of
death.[5]

Jews always have the opportunity to turn to God's antidote to the
evil inclination, the Torah and its laws, in addition to the tool of prayer.
The very act of studying Torah will, according to the rabbis, enable a
person to combat and even temporarily defeat the power and seduction
of the evil inclination. God did not leave people alone for a lifetime of
struggle with the inclination, destined to repeat failure, submission and
sin in a never-ending cycle. God implanted the inclination in us so that
people would struggle and God also gave the Torah and prayer so that
we would not face the challenge unarmed:

Even so did the Holy One of Blessing
speak to Israel, "My children, I created
the *yetzer hara*, but I (also) created the
Torah as its antidote. If you occupy
yourselves with the Torah, you will not
be delivered into its (the *yetzer hara's*)
hand....But if you do not occupy
yourselves with the Torah, you shall
be delivered into his hand....He is
completely preoccupied with you...yet
if you will, you can rule over him....
Rabbi Isaac said, "Man's *yetzer hara*
renews itself daily against him....And
Rabbi Simeon ben Levi said, "Man's
yetzer hara gathers strength against
him daily and seeks to kill him...and

were not the Holy One of Blessing
to help him, he would not be able to
prevail against him.[6]

Only humans, possessing an evil inclination implanted by God, need the Torah to combat the pull of the inclination. Angels, who have no capacity for evil, have no need for Torah. When the angels protest giving the Torah to imperfect, sinful humans, among God's responses is one that makes clear that Torah, specifically the commandments against murder, adultery and stealing, is how humans combat the evil inclination. God's laws, the rabbis teach, are the barrier between us and sinful behavior:

Is there jealousy among you (angels),
is the *yetzer hara* among you (that you
would need the Torah and its laws)?
Right away they conceded to the Holy
One of Blessing.[7]

When the rabbis refer to Torah as an antidote to the evil inclination they are including the implied understanding that it is the study of Torah and the obedience to its laws that flows from that study that helps a person to manage his evil inclination. Doing God's commandments, the *mitzvot*, is what will enable a person to follow the good rather than evil inclination. In this spirit, an elaborate allegorical interpretation is made of the sheep, well and stone of Genesis 29:2f ("There before his eyes was a well in the open. Three flocks of sheep were lying there beside it, for the flocks were watered from that well. The stone on the mouth of the well was large. When all the flocks were gathered there, the stone would be rolled from the mouth of the well and the sheep watered; then the stone would be put back in its place on the mouth of the well."):

> "And behold a well in the field,"
> symbolizes the synagogue. "And three
> flocks of sheep," represent the three
> men called (to the public reading of
> the Torah). "For out of that well,"
> represents where they heard the Torah.
> "And the stone was great," symbolizes
> the *yetzer hara*. "And all the flocks
> were gathered there," represents the
> congregation. "The stone would be
> rolled," represents the hearing of the
> Torah. "Then the stone would be
> put back,"—as soon as they leave the
> synagogue the *yetzer hara* returns to its
> place.[8]

Hearing the words of Torah, being reminded of God's words and laws, removes the evil inclination from the listener's spirit, but the antidote is fleeting as the inclination returns to its place as soon as the words are no longer being heard. This would argue for a person constantly being immersed in words of Torah to experience long-lasting success in fending off the influence of the evil inclination. Unfortunately a person is not able to be immersed constantly in studying Torah, so the power of the antidote is always temporary and fleeting. The principle the rabbis are enunciating is that the more one can spend time studying Torah, the more lasting is the power to manage and control the evil inclination.

In the context of a broad discussion of the evil forces God created, i.e. Satan, the evil inclination and the angel of death, the fact of Torah's role as antidote to the inclination is made succinctly:

> If God created the *yetzer hara* He also
> created the Torah as its antidote.[9]

> The *yetzer hara* has no power in the
> presence of Torah. And so the *yetzer
> hara* has no power over him who has
> Torah in his heart, and cannot touch
> him.[10]

The expectation that people can and will use the laws of Torah to guard against the desires of the evil inclination is spelled out explicitly in commentary referring to the epic battle between Torah and the evil inclination:

> The Holy One of Blessing said, "The
> Torah is called a stone and the *yetzer
> hara* is called a stone." So the Torah is
> a stone and the *yetzer hara* is a stone;
> the stone shall watch the stone.[11]

The Torah does not vanquish or destroy the evil inclination, but is vigilant over it. They are depicted as two stones, both durable and strong, and the function of Torah is to guard against the urges of the inclination. The rabbis suggest here that the Torah and the evil inclination are of similar strength, that this is a battle between equals. God, after all, created both. This text supports the sense expressed typically by the rabbis that the struggle between the forces of the evil inclination and the Torah is a struggle that must be waged, that can be won, at least in the short term, but which requires all the strength one can muster.

This tool of Torah, with which Jews can do battle with the evil inclination is one that often appears to be separate from the people, a tool they can reach for periodically, but which does not reside in their spirit. Commenting on Song of Songs 1:2, "Let him kiss me with the kisses of his mouth," the Midrash expresses the idea that God put the knowledge of the Torah and the evil inclination in the hearts of the Israelites and the two contend for a place in their spirits:

> When the Israelites heard the words
> (in the Ten Commandments), "I am
> the Lord your God," the knowledge of
> Torah was fixed in their heart and they
> learned and did not forget....Rabbi
> Nechemiah said, "When Israel heard
> the command, "You shall not have
> any gods before Me (Exodus 20:3),"
> the *yetzer hara* was plucked from their
> heart. They came to Moses and said to
> him, "Our master Moses, you become
> an intermediary between us...What
> profit is there in our perishing?" Right
> away the *yetzer hara* returned to its
> place. They returned to Moses and
> said to him, "Moses, would that God
> would reveal himself to us a second
> time. Would that he would kiss us
> 'with the kisses of his mouth.'" He
> replied to them, "This cannot be now,
> but in time to come it will be."[12]

This complex passage speaks to the question of the contending presence of the Torah and the evil inclination in the hearts of the Israelites and their struggle with those battling forces. The Torah is available as the tool in the fight with the evil inclination, but the inclination is not going away quietly. In this passage, closeness to God brings a person enduring knowledge of Torah and the temporary defeat of the adversary. The rabbis here are suggesting that Jews continue to live in a state of distance from God in this world, allowing the evil inclination to live with, even within them. The people's desire to have Moses function as an intermediary between them and God speaks to the sinful desire of the people for distance from God. This situation of the people living subject to the power of the evil inclination, as we have seen previously, will only change in the future to come, in the time of ultimate redemption. This midrash serves both as an attack on having an intermediary between the individual Jew and God and the ultimate power of God's Torah to vanquish the evil inclination. It seems that the power of Torah or even God to defeat the evil inclination can only be transitory in this world and will only be fully realized in the time to come.

A person can find refuge from the evil inclination in a place of Torah, specifically a place in which people are studying Torah, a House of Study. The inclination cannot even enter a place where people are engaged in studying Torah and so taking refuge there will enable anyone to fight off its enticements. Even for a person as prominent as King David, perhaps especially for him given his history with Bat Sheva, the body wants to follow the ways of the evil inclination and only in taking refuge with Torah can that desire be resisted:

> David said, "Do not let my feet go wherever they want to, but only to Your Torah. Make them go for all the day into the *Bet Midrash* (House of Study), for the *yetzer hara* does not enter there. The *yetzer hara* walks with a man all the way, but when he reaches the house of study, it does not have the power to enter. Thus Torah says, "Sin lies at the door." (Genesis 4:7) When a man occupies himself with Torah, the *yetzer hara* has no power over him.[13]

The evil inclination is present in everyone except for the singularly, stellar righteous of the Bible and everyone else contends with the competing forces of the good and evil inclinations implanted within us by God. The stellar righteous of the Bible are apparently so constitutionally infused with Torah and God's laws that they do not have to engage in the struggle. God has implanted the evil inclination in humans so people will procreate and produce and God has given people the antidote, the laws of Torah, so that they can manage and control the urges of the inclination. The evil inclination, then, makes people fully human, beings able to choose between good and evil. Adherence to God's laws enables people to resist the evil pull of the inclination that draws people away from God.

What we have looked at in this review of rabbinic literature on the evil inclination are isolated passages, some brief, some more extensive. These passages have enabled us to piece together an understanding of how the rabbis understood the power and origin of the evil inclination as well as the solution to the problem, Torah and its laws. As we saw in the Bible with Solomon's prayer (I Kings 8) there is in rabbinic literature one text that comprehensively describes the topic of sin and the evil inclination. In rabbinic literature we find it in an exhaustive sermon in the midrashic text, *Pesikta deRav Kahana*. This ancient midrash, apparently written in the Land of Israel as early as the sixth century CE and ascribed to Rav Kahana, includes homilies focusing on holiday celebrations and biblical texts. In this midrash we find a supplementary chapter 3, ascribed to Rabbi Nathan. There is nothing new here, and in fact it could be seen as a summary, or synthesis of the major themes of rabbinic literature regarding the evil inclination.

We read of the essential nature of the inclination, its particular qualities as the older and stronger force than the good inclination, and how it leads to sexual misbehavior. It begins with a verse from Ecclesiastes (4:13), "Better is a poor and wise child than an old and foolish king who no longer has the sense to heed warnings, For the former can emerge from a dungeon to become king, while the latter even if born to kingship can become a pauper." As we have seen in other rabbinic midrash texts on the same passage, the king is seen as a metaphor for the evil inclination because the king, like the evil inclination, has the power to rule over humans and direct their behavior. The child represents the good inclination because it only appears when people reach the age of thirteen years "and only then begins to guide them in the right path."[14] We read in this sermon that the evil inclination is, as we have seen before, essential to human functioning and that it endures after the later emergence of the good inclination. Appearing when a person is thirteen years old, the good inclination is seen as young, but wise, since it knows the proper path for human behavior.

As we have seen elsewhere in rabbinic literature, here in this sermon the rabbis explain how the evil inclination drives people to act out sexually. The sermon encourages us to understand the powerful strength of the evil inclination. In this context the sermon then cites three righteous people of Jewish tradition, Joseph in the Bible and two rabbinic sages and explains how they resisted the power of the evil inclination. The sermon, after detailing how these righteous men managed to resist the power of the evil inclination, offers a cautionary note to the reader: lest you think you can do what these three did, do not discount the powerful pull of the evil inclination. Their ability to resist it speaks to their distinctive righteousness, not any weakness in the inclination or to the likelihood that the rest of us can do the same.

The sermon warns the reader that the evil inclination is with us from our very birth, causing a baby to reach for a hot coal, and that it can only be resisted with the fiery words of Torah. In its final portion, the sermon lays out the only possible solution to the urges caused by the evil inclination. Repentance is the key strategy available to any person who finds himself submitting to the inclination. We read of a wall around the prison in which the evil inclination can trap people, and repentance is a breech in the wall. Repentance is the escape route that will free us from the prison of the evil inclination. The evil inclination seeks to trap us in its prison of sin and God has provided two paths for escape—heed the laws of Torah and when we do fail in that endeavor and succumb to the temptations of sin, repentance will free us.

In this one midrashic sermon we see that the rabbis believed we live our lives with this evil inclination implanted in us by God and that there is a struggle within us between the two inclinations for control over our actions. People are not, in the rabbinic view, inherently evil, but creatures who by their very nature must choose between good and evil. The evil inclination is strong and durable, a veritable brigand within the human spirit. God has not, however, left us to fend for our lives alone, but has provided us with prayer, Torah and repentance. It is left to us how we will manage the struggle and whether we will employ the strategies provided by God in the struggle that defines our humanity.

1. Midrash, Pesikta deRab Kahana 23.7

2. Talmud, Berachot 17a

3. The Sh'ma is often referred to as the "Watchword of Our Faith," and is considered the central declaration of Jewish faith in one God. The Sh'ma itself is Deuteronomy 6:5, "Hear O Israel, the Lord our God is One." The bedtime recitation of Sh'ma, known in Hebrew as *k'riat Sh'ma*, consists of those opening words, the succeeding verses and other liturgical texts.

4. Talmud, Berachot 60b

5. Talmud, Berachot 5a

6. Talmud, Kiddushin 30b

7. Talmud, Shabbat 89a

8. Midrash, Genesis Rabbah 70.8

9. Talmud, Baba Batra 16a

10. Midrash, Psalms Rabbah 119.7

11. Midrash Leviticus Rabbah 35.5

12. Midrash Song of Songs Rabbah 1.2.4

13. Midrash Psalms Rabbah 119.64

14. Pesikta deRav Kahana supplementary chapter 3

CHAPTER 6   PAUL AND AUGUSTINE ON THE ORIGIN AND NATURE OF SIN

Among the earliest and most important followers of Jesus of Nazareth in the first century CE was Paul of Tarsus. Born a Jew named Saul, he was apparently inclined to persecute and rhetorically attack those in the Jewish community who believed Jesus was the awaited messiah. Paul experienced the famous conversion on the road to Damascus while on an assignment to scout out and possibly imprison followers of Jesus. He became devoted to Jesus as a result of his vision on the road and wrote, evangelized and taught from the 40s to the time of his death in the mid-60s of the first century. He faced the same problem with sin as the rabbis—what would compel people, in such consistent and persistent fashion, to think and act contrary to God's expectations. As we will see, for Paul, the construct for understanding sin was not the rabbis' formulation of an evil inclination, and the solution for human sinfulness is dramatically different. How could we account for the tendency of humans to engage in sinful acts, especially in the context of their belief that they were created by God? Belief in a creator God who is good and our acute awareness of the human condition compels people of faith to account for the existence of human sinfulness.

In this chapter the focus will be on the writing of Paul in the book of Romans in the New Testament and the writings a few centuries later of St. Augustine. This seminal Christian thinker and writer, living in North Africa from 354-430 CE, became much more than the Bishop of Hippo. Despite the fact that some people reject particulars of his thinking and writing in modern times, he is the single most important Christian thinker of the early centuries of church history. His primary writings dealing with the issue of sin are *The City of God* and the intensely personal *Confessions*.

Paul's letters preserved as part of the New Testament are among the oldest Christian documents, apparently written in the middle of the first century, about twenty-five years after the death of Jesus. The Book of Romans is a discourse on Paul's part regarding this new faith, laying out for the reader key elements of the faith he is promulgating. He tries to show the reader how his faith in Jesus diverges from traditional Judaism and what one has to believe to be a follower of Jesus. He shows how his faith is rooted in Judaism but is now a faith for all humanity. Paul's full treatment of his theological foundation provides a thorough insight into the dimensions of his faith and in chapters six and seven of Romans we read his views on the sinful nature of man.

Paul sets up a balance between Adam and Jesus on the issue of human sinfulness. Adam introduced sinfulness and death into the human character when he ate the fruit of the tree of knowledge of good and evil and Jesus came to bring forgiveness and everlasting life. In between the two, Moses came to introduce law, increasing sinfulness and making even more pressing the need for Jesus and the free gift of grace, or forgiveness:

> Therefore, just as sin entered the
> world through one man (Adam),
> and death through sin, and in this

way death came to all men, because
all sinned—for before the law was
given, sin was in the world. But sin is
not taken into account when there is
no law. Nevertheless, death reigned
from the time of Adam to the time
of Moses, even over those who did
not sin by breaking a command, as
did Adam, who was a pattern of the
one to come…Consequently, just as
one man's (Adam's) trespass led to
condemnation for all, so one man's
(Jesus') act of righteousness leads to
justification and life for all. For just
as by the one man's disobedience the
many were made sinners, so by the
one man's obedience the many will be
made righteous. But law came in, with
the result that the trespass multiplied;
but where sin increased, grace
abounded all the more, so that, just
as sin exercised dominion in death,
so grace might also exercise dominion
through justification leading to eternal
life through Jesus Christ our Lord.[1]

Here Paul suggests the doctrine we will see in much more elaborate form in Augustine regarding the origin of human sinfulness. It was the act of Adam (and Eve presumably), violating God's commandment regarding the forbidden fruit of the Garden of Eden, that introduced sinfulness in human character. Paul never calls it Original Sin, but it is the foundation of the idea that God did not make humans sinful. The first human introduced sin into human character through the disobedient choice he made. It was a willful act of this first human that made subsequent humans sinful or at least inclined to sin. Subsequent humans either ratify Adam's act and commit our own personal sins or we consent to Jesus' act through our faith. According to Paul the result of our choice to sin is that we will die and the consequence of our faith in Jesus is everlasting life.

Paul deals much more extensively with how we deal with our sinful nature than with the origin of that sinfulness. Most of his writings on the subject of human sinfulness are quite different in context from that of the rabbis of Talmud and Midrash, but he does agree that people have to exercise control over this part of their personality. Where he differs, quite extensively and fundamentally, is the role of law in enabling a person to take control over his or her sinfulness:

> Therefore, do not let sin exercise
> dominion in your mortal bodies, to
> make you obey their passions…For sin
> will have no dominion over you, since
> you are not under law but under grace.
> What then? Should we sin because we
> are not under the law but under grace?
> By no means![2]

For the rabbis of the generations after Paul, the antidote to the evil inclination is God's law, the tool God has provided people to take control of and rule over the urge to sin. For Paul the law is most decidedly not an antidote and in fact it is completely futile in helping one to avoid sinfulness. The law was at best merely the bridge from the faith of Abraham to the coming of the savior, Jesus. In lieu of the law, it is grace as a result of faith in Jesus that washes away sin:

> Since all have sinned and fall short
> of the glory of God; they are now
> justified by his grace as a gift, through
> the redemption that is in Christ Jesus,

whom God put forward as a sacrifice
of atonement by his blood, effective
through faith.[3]

Under the law, or Torah, we were slaves to sin and now, after the
sacrificial death of Jesus, his followers are "slaves to righteousness."[4]
Paul wrote that those who are faithful to Jesus are liberated from the
law and that faith frees people from sinful passions. Paul went on to
contend that it is the law itself that prompted people to sinfulness:

> While we were living in the flesh,
> our sinful passions, aroused by the
> law, were at work in our members to
> bear fruit for death. But now we are
> discharged from the law, dead to that
> which held us captive, so that we are
> slaves not under the old written code
> but in the new life of the spirit.[5]

Paul holds a view that is the complete opposite of the rabbinic view
of the relationship between law and sin:

> If it had not been for the law, I would
> not have known sin. I would not have
> known what it is to covet if the law
> had not said, 'You shall not covet.'…
> apart from the law sin lies dead.[6]

In Paul's writings, sin seems to have a life of its own and that life
is derived from, given breath by, the laws and commandments of
the Torah. Paul is suggesting that were it not for these laws of Jewish
antiquity people would not have sinned. He points out that before
the law was given, Abraham was a man of faith whose righteousness
accrued to him not due to his adherence to law, but because of his faith
which preceded the giving of the law. The rabbinic tradition later deals

with this question of Abraham and the law by holding that even though the law had not been given yet, Abraham still followed its precepts. For Paul's purposes, it is important to note that Abraham is acknowledged as righteous before he is ever seen as adhering to any of God's laws:

> What then are we to say was gained
> by Abraham, our ancestor according
> to the flesh? For if Abraham was
> justified by works, he has something
> to boast about, but not before God.
> For what does scripture say? 'Abraham
> believed God, and it was reckoned
> to him as righteousness.'…We say,
> 'Faith was reckoned to Abraham as
> righteousness.' How then was it
> reckoned to him? Was it before or after
> he had been circumcised? It was not
> after, but before he was circumcised.
> He received the sign of circumcision
> as a seal of the righteousness that
> he had by faith while he was still
> uncircumcised. The purpose was to
> make him the ancestor of all who
> believe without being circumcised and
> who thus have righteousness reckoned
> to them.[7]

In rejecting the need for physical circumcision, Paul is rejecting the outward sign of the historic Jewish covenant with God. For Paul, circumcision was merely the seal of a righteousness that Abraham had already achieved based on his faith in God. In Romans Paul writes that Abraham represents universal man, reckoned for righteousness because of faith, regardless of adherence to the law. Paul has great motivation for this characterization and for his rejection of the need for adherence to the law, as he is working to universalize the faith in Jesus, promoting the faith to non-Jews. They can, according to Paul, be deemed to be righteous through their faith in the purported messiah without adherence to Jewish law. This becomes a major sticking point in his relations with the rest of the Jewish community and becomes the beginning of a divide between the Jewish followers of Jesus and those Jews who do not see him as the messiah. Paul is arguing that one can be a follower, and thus presumably in his historic context, Jewish, without circumcision or adherence to the rest of Mosaic law. The gentiles, according to Paul, need not come to Jesus through the laws of Judaism, just as Abraham, according to Paul, did not come to God through the laws.

In Paul's writings in Romans, sin lives in the realm of flesh, in the very physicality of human existence. He writes of the flesh as the abode of sin and sets up the duality of flesh and soul, the latter being the dwelling place of human righteousness and goodness. Since sinfulness resides in the flesh, a person is compelled to sin even if and when s/he does not want to do it. It is as if the person has no control over his/her own sinfulness:

> But in fact it is no longer I that do
> it, but sin that dwells with me. For I
> know that nothing good dwells within
> me, that is in my flesh. I can will what
> is right, but I cannot do it. For I do
> not do the good I want, but the evil I
> do not want is what I do. Now if I do
> what I do not want, it is no longer I
> that do it, but sin that dwells within
> me. So I find it to be a law that when I
> want to do what is good, evil lies close
> at hand.[8]

He offers a succinct juxtaposition of the role of body and mind in the context of a person's sinful character, "So then, with my mind I am a slave to the law of God, but with my flesh I am a slave to the law of sin."[9] In this writing Paul personifies sin as a nearly independent force that resides within the individual's physical being.

In Paul's doctrine of the sinful character of humans, the law entices a person to sin and faith in Jesus frees us from the consequences of our sinful nature. Faith and Jesus' sacrifice do not free us from committing sin, but enable us to experience the grace of God's forgiveness. Paul's teaching holds that God sent and sacrificed his son, God in the flesh, so that his suffering and death would provide forgiveness for those who believe in him. Human physicality is the dwelling place of sin and the spirit of faith liberates us from the aftermath or consequences of sin. He sets up a conflict between law and physicality on one hand and faith and spirit on the other. Sin has an independent existence from human will and can only be defeated through faith.

Augustine lived three hundred years after Paul and is the heir to the vast body of Christian writing and thinking in the intervening centuries. He was a contemporary of the Jewish sages of the Talmud and Midrash but there is no evidence of his being aware of their writings or thought. Augustine is presumably well aware of Paul's writings and builds on the theological positions of his predecessor, the great disseminator of the faith. Augustine is viewed by many as a bridge between the ancient world of the East and the modern world of the West, at least as regards theology and faith. It has been said of this North African mystic, "St. Augustine's view of history is the view held by the Catholic Church."[10] Extensively in *The City of God*, and to a lesser extent in *The Confessions*, Augustine lays out his view of man's sinfulness, its origin and how one controls and defeats it.

Augustine takes the view put forth centuries before by the Greek philosopher, Aristotle, that there are pure forms of good and evil and that God can only be associated with pure good. In a discussion of angels and man he describes his view of how beings can be good and evil:

> Since God, the good Author and
> Creator of all essences, created them
> both, but from a difference in their
> wills and desires, it is impossible to
> doubt…The cause therefore, of the
> blessedness of the good is adherence to
> God. And so the cause of the others'
> misery will be found in the contrary,
> that is, in their not adhering to God.
> Wherefore, if when the question is
> asked, why are the former (angels)
> blessed, it is rightly answered, because
> they adhere to God; and when it is
> asked, why are the latter (humans)
> miserable, it is rightly answered,
> because they do not adhere to God.[11]

Augustine also holds that there is a natural, or eternal, law that supercedes codes of law man creates and follows. This eternal law is associated in his thinking with reason and anything consistent with it is right and good by definition. When an action is not in harmony with eternal law it is evil and when man's free will, independent of God's desires, enters it is sinful. Adhering to the reason of eternal law leads one to good behavior and when we follow our senses and desires we are led to sin. Sin then, for Augustine, is a disruption of the natural order of man and sin upsets his order of being. Sin is always contrary to reason. Passion, ignorance or a lustful appetite for sensual desires are sinful and a perversion of the judgment of reason. "Sin is man's inordinate movement toward a goal chosen by himself."[12]

In Augustine's view, while man is created good, he inherits a will from Adam and Eve that perverts his natural essence and this will leads him to inordinately desire the material necessities of life. Everyone has to have food, drink, and sex to live but it is when people desire these necessities too much that a person sins. The will to possess is the problem in human behavior and it is the motivator of action we take to acquire the desired object. That action is inevitably sinful. "Man chooses a passing good at the price of eternal happiness."[13] We have a natural inclination to be virtuous and we can be distracted or perverted by habitual sin.

Pride and covetousness are, for Augustine, the underlying causes of people's sinful behavior. Pride leads us toward an inordinate desire to excel, achieve and acquire and covetousness moves us to the desire to have things beyond what reason would dictate. If we could only desire material things within the bounds of what we need and what reason dictates we would not sin. Augustine argues that living in pursuit of the flesh, of the material world is evil, even though the flesh itself cannot be evil because it is created by God. It is the carnal *desires* of living in the realm of the flesh that leads to evil behavior. In his view there are two kinds of men, those who, "live after the flesh, the other of those who wish to live after the spirit."[14]

The evil will, the closest Augustine comes to identifying a human component of personality that approximates the evil inclination, cannot have any positive purpose or function:

> If the further question be asked,
> 'What was the efficient cause of their
> evil will?' there is none. For what is it
> which makes the will bad, when it is
> the will itself which makes the action
> bad? And consequently the bad will
> is the cause of the bad action, but
> nothing is the efficient cause of the
> bad will.[15]

If by "efficient cause," we understand Augustine to mean the purpose of the bad will, he is suggesting that there is no good purpose for a bad will and it has no positive end. Augustine believed that sin serves no positive purpose and is man's rebellion against the good nature with which man was created by God:

> Evil enters the world, it persists, but
> it consists of nothing more than the
> perversity of dependent creatures,
> fleetingly anonymous in their
> rebellion. Through sin, death and
> all misery entered the world. The
> wounds of life are all self-inflicted.[16]

Augustine argues that when man succumbs to his physicality, refusing to rise up to his spiritual existence, he succumbs to his sinfulness:

> The will is bound not by the flesh, but
> by its own misuse of the flesh...Thus
> it is not the body and the flesh but the
> habituated will, willing in and through
> the flesh, that binds man in the law of
> sin...The flesh cannot lust unless the
> soul lusts in and through it; nor can
> it be corrupted unless the soul is first
> corrupted.[17]

He offers a comprehensive view of the nature and origin of the evil will and uses the hypothetical example of two men who see a beautiful woman. In his example, one man succumbs to the evil will upon seeing the woman and the other does not. In accounting for the difference he offers his view of how the evil will functions. The men are inherently or naturally good as creatures of God, but one acts on an evil will which does not and cannot derive from God:

We can discern nothing which caused
the will of the one to be evil. For if we
say that the man himself made his will
evil, what was the man himself before
his will was evil but a good nature
created by God, the unchangeable
good? Here are two men who, before
the temptation, were alike in body and
soul, and of whom one yielded to the
tempter who persuaded him, while the
other could not be persuaded to desire
that lovely body which was equally
before the eyes of both. Shall we say of
the successfully tempted man that he
corrupted his own will, since he was
certainly good before his will became
bad? Then, why did he do so? Was
it because his will was a nature, or
because it was made of nothing? We
shall find that the latter is the case.[18]

The impulse to sin must be a defect not in the nature of the human
created by God, but a corruption that came about by human action.
God can only create something good, "This I do know, that the nature
of God can never, nowhere, nowise be defective, and that natures made
of nothing can."[19]

Augustine also believes in the existence of the devil, the one who
brings evil into the lives of men; it is the devil who prompts men to
sin:

For though we cannot call the devil
a fornicator or drunkard, or ascribe
to him any sensual indulgence
(though he is the secret instigator and
prompter of those who sin in these

ways)…When man lives according to
man, not according to God, he is like
the devil.[20]

In this view of the nature of man and his sinfulness, man consists
of flesh and soul or spirit and he has to choose between the two, to
decide whether he will follow the desires of the flesh or those of the
soul. If he is devoted to God he will follow the desires of the spirit and
if not he will follow the desires of the flesh. The ultimate good then is
denying the desires or pleasures of the flesh and Augustine identifies
the chief among these to be sexuality. Abstinence is the ultimate good,
the choice of the spirit over the flesh and it is the only way to avoid
following the desires of the flesh and therefore sinfulness.

Augustine also presents a doctrine that is preserved in Christian
thought to this day, separating a person's sinful acts from the person
himself. He puts forth the notion that one should hate the sin but love
the sinner:

> Wherefore the man who lives
> according to God, and not according
> to man, ought to be a lover of good,
> and therefore a hater of evil. And since
> no one is evil by nature, but whoever
> is evil is evil by vice, he who lives
> according to God ought to cherish
> towards evil men a perfect hatred,
> so that he shall neither hate the man
> because of his vice, nor love the vice
> because of the man, but hate the vice
> and love the man.[21]

The good will of man comes from God and, as we have seen, the
evil comes from outside God's creation:

Accordingly to God, as it is written He
made man upright, and consequently
with a good will…the good will, then
is the work of God; for God created
him with it. But the first evil will,
which preceded all man's evil acts, was
rather a kind of falling away from the
work of God to its own works than
any positive work.[22]

There is, in Augustine's writing, no discussion of an internal
struggle between the forces of good and evil, but the presumption of
an essential goodness imparted by God as creator and the evil that was
introduced by Adam's defiance of God in the Garden of Eden. Man
chooses between the two, but Augustine does not account for any kind
of internal struggle.

The doctrine of Original Sin plays a major part in Augustine's
writings, and in fact he is largely credited with introducing the idea
to Christianity and Western thought. The doctrine holds that we
humans fell from the basic goodness with which God created us in the
sin of Adam in the Garden, making all of us sinners, capable of sin.
Insubordination or rebellion against God is the root of Original Sin
and it is a condition inherited by all people (except for Jesus' mother,
Mary). The natural order of man, God's gift of original justice, was lost
through the rebellion of Adam and Eve and in lieu of original justice
we live now with Original Sin. We cannot, according to Augustine,
lose that natural state of goodness, but its hold over us is diminished
as a result of our inheritance of Adam and Eve's disobedient act. Our
nature is wounded and the natural order of life is disrupted. Death,
suffering and bodily defects are the result of Original Sin and too often
we become accustomed to sinful choices and sin becomes habitual.

We still choose whether to commit the sin or not. Augustine does
not believe that man is a blank slate, poised between good and evil,

compelled to choose between contending internal forces implanted by God. He believes that:

> All men and women start with a
> handicap. Even when the eternal
> consequences of Original Sin are
> removed by baptism, it still affects
> the soul so that every human being
> eventually succumbs to sin.[23]

He therefore holds that while man is naturally good, he has become sinful as a result of his inheritance of Original Sin based on Adam's rebellion against God. Given that state, we are in need of God's grace:

> Augustine taught that mankind
> since Adam is always and everywhere
> subject to inherited concupiscence
> and sin....the absolute gratuity and
> necessity of grace for salvation reveals
> the depths of man's sin.[24]

Augustine connected the idea of Original Sin to concupiscence, the human's desire for physical or sensual pleasure. This lust is transmitted through sexual intercourse and so associated with each human from the very procreative act of the parents. "To the extent that concupiscence infects every human act, all of our deeds are in some sense sinful."[25]

Augustine wrote *The Confessions* in 399 CE and in this intensely personal document he accounts for his own sinfulness and his subsequent understanding of the nature and origin of that sinfulness. At one point he discusses his own adolescent lustfulness and the refusal of his parents to have him married as a way to channel those desires. He then turns to his acts of theft as a youth and the fact that his desire to steal (fruit) came from the fact that the act was forbidden, not because he desired the object itself:

> I loved the evil in me—not the thing
> for which I did the evil, simply the
> evil: my soul was depraved, and
> hurled itself down from security in
> you into utter destruction, seeking no
> profit from wickedness but only to be
> wicked.[26]

For Augustine, the desire people have for material wealth is itself evil, independent of the nature of the thing desired; lack of moderation in the pursuit of material goods is a root of evil:

> Yet in the enjoyment of all such things
> we commit sin if through immoderate
> inclination to them—for though they
> are good, they are of the lowest order
> of good—things higher and better are
> forgotten, even You, O Lord our God,
> and your truth and Law.[27]

Material things and their pursuit distract a person from God and God's truth and so they are the "lowest order of good."

Sin is inevitable because we inherit Original Sin from Adam and all his descendants. God created us naturally good, but Adam's disobedience infused us with a sinful character. But we are still responsible for the sins we commit because while we inherit Original Sin we still have the choice whether to sin or not. Augustine holds that baptism in the faith and life of Christ frees a person from the consequences of sin. Building on the writings of Paul and the early church fathers, Augustine teaches that faith in Jesus and his sacrifice on our behalf offers us forgiveness for the sins we commit. A person's acts do not provide forgiveness, faith in Jesus does.

Augustine saw the "history of the species as a struggle with sin brought to an end only when divine goodness intervenes and liberates men for eternity."[28]

1. Romans 5:12-21

2. ibid., 6:12ff

3. ibid., 3:23

4. ibid., 6:18

5. ibid., 7:5f

6. ibid., 7:7

7. ibid., 4:1ff

8. ibid., 7:17ff

9. ibid., 7:25

10. Merton, Introduction to The City of God, ix.

11. ibid., Book Twelfth, 380.

12. Snell, 51.

13. ibid., 52

14. ibid., Book Fourteenth, 441

15. Merton, Book Twelfth, 385.

16. O'Donnell, 63.

17. Rigby, 77.

18. Merton, Book Twelfth, 386.

19. ibid., 387

20. ibid., 444f

21. ibid., 448

22. ibid., 451

23. O'Donnell, 64.

24. Rigby, 11.

25. McBrien, 187.

26. Augustine, <u>The Confessions of Augustine</u>, Book Two, Chapter IV, 32.

27. ibid.

28. O'Donnell, 64.

CHAPTER 7   THOMAS AQUINAS AND MARTIN LUTHER ON SIN

Christian thought and doctrine regarding sin and human nature begins with Paul, Augustine and other early leaders of the church but it certainly does not end there. Scholars, thinkers and philosophers have made great contributions to the body of Christian thinking on these topics. We will turn our attention now to two Christian thinkers from about one thousand years after Paul and Augustine. Thomas Aquinas and Martin Luther each had a major influence on Christian thought on various topics, including the question of sin and human nature.

Thomas Aquinas was born in 1225 in Aquino, Italy and died in 1274.[1] Over the objections of his family he became a Dominican priest and distinguished himself as a brilliant scholar early in life. As a young man he received a Doctor of Theology degree from the University of Paris. He studied with one of the leading scholars of his day, Albert Magnus, in Cologne, Germany; it was Magnus who upon hearing Aquinas' defense of his doctoral thesis said, "We call this young man a dumb ox, but his bellowing in doctrine will one day resound throughout the world." His humility and reticence to shine earned him the unfortunate nickname, "dumb ox," but Magnus surely described his ultimate impact on Christian doctrine accurately.

Aquinas' major work was *Summa Theologica*, his commentary to a theology textbook. In it and his other writings he expounded on numerous theological and philosophical issues, including the question of human nature and sin. By the thirteenth century the doctrine of Original Sin had become central to Christian doctrine and anyone who wanted to comment on the nature of sin would have to focus his comments on this doctrine. For Aquinas, "Original Sin is…an 'illness' which, though it weakens and injures human nature, does not render human nature ugly or radically perverse."[2] In Aquinas' writings, Original Sin is the counter-point to Original Justice. The latter refers to the manner in which God created humanity, the "wonderfully ordered state of man."[3] Aquinas holds that man is created in an orderly state in which he is subject to God, and animals are subject to man. God intended that man would hand down this state of Original Justice to his descendants as part of human nature. Original Justice meant that man would, by nature, obey God's commands and follow God's will. When we read in Genesis about Adam and Eve eating the prohibited fruit, Aquinas understands that the eating of the fruit was evil simply because it was forbidden. "By eating of it," Aquinas writes, "man learned by experience the difference between the good of obedience and the evil of disobedience."[4]

As Paul states in I Corinthians 15:21f, Aquinas argues that the result of man's disobedience in the Garden eating the fruit is the introduction of death into the human experience.[5] The presence of sin leads directly to the inevitability of suffering and death. Adam's disobedience also led directly, Aquinas states, to the withdrawal of Original Justice from humanity.

Therefore, when the first man stripped
himself of this good by his sin, all his
descendants were likewise deprived of
it. And so for all time—that is, ever
since the sin of the first parent—all
men come into the world bereft of
Original Justice and burdened with
the defects that attend its loss.[6]

Aquinas holds that it is called Original Sin because it is transmitted from the first parent to his descendants and it is the perversion of the natural state of Original Justice. The sins a person commits affect only the person who commits them while Original Sin is passed down through the generations of humans from Adam and Eve. The sins we commit ourselves are not transmitted, only this state of Original Sin is passed on from the first people to all of humanity.

Aquinas writes of sin in contexts other than Original Sin. He writes about sin extensively in the context of grace, the gift of man's union with or connection to God. He holds that "sins arise when actions deflect from the right course leading to the end…and must be counteracted…by the help which grace confers…Sins are forgiven by the gifts of grace."[7] Aquinas writes that man is naturally good and that sins are a corruption of that natural state and man requires the gift of grace to be forgiven for those sins we inevitably commit. He goes on to argue that only God can forgive sin since sin is an offense against God.[8]

In this brief overview of the thought of Thomas Aquinas on the subject of sin we see that he has built upon the foundation provided by Paul and Augustine before him, elaborating on the idea of Original Sin. He believes that man is created with a perfectly good nature by a God incapable of anything else and defines man's natural state as one of Original Justice. Humans corrupted this state by disobeying God in the Garden of Eden, introducing the reality of Original Sin as an inherited state passed on down through the generations. God alone can forgive the sin through the gift of grace and man is restored to his original state through the incarnation of God as Jesus. Aquinas teaches that there is a completed circle from Original Justice to Original Sin to the personal commission of sin to grace through Jesus Christ. Man is good, man inherits a sinful state, man sins and man is forgiven through the grace of God.

The German priest and theologian, Martin Luther, was born two and a half centuries after Aquinas (1483-1546) and wages a great ideological battle with the Catholic church. Luther challenges the authenticity of the papacy and wages war with the church over indulgences, the importance of studying the Bible, especially in the vernacular, the role of the priest and much more. While he offers some distinctive thoughts on the question of salvation, he does not break new ground on the question of sin and human nature.

Luther embraces the idea of Original Sin, which has become normative theology for Christianity by the fifteenth century. He writes frequently about humans as sinners and makes one of his strongest assertions on the question of sin:

> If you are a preacher of Grace, then
> preach a true, not a fictitious grace;
> if grace is true, you must bear a true
> and not a fictitious sin. God does not
> save people who are only fictitious
> sinners. Be a sinner and sin boldly,
> but believe and rejoice in Christ even
> more boldly. For he is victorious over
> sin, death, and the world. As long as
> we are here we have to sin. This life is
> not the dwelling place of righteousness
> but, as Peter says, we look for a new
> heaven and a new earth in which
> righteousness dwells. . . . Pray boldly--
> you too are a mighty sinner.[9]

It is a typically provocative statement for Luther: "Be a sinner and sin boldly." He wants people to know that if they have faith in Jesus and in his forgiving grace they can afford to sin boldly. Their fervent faith in Jesus will bring them forgiveness "over sin, death and the world." If sin is inevitable, and Luther certainly believes that it is, then believers have to know that they will be forgiven. He seems to be suggesting that if we try to avoid sinning it is as if we do not have strong enough faith in Jesus' grace to save us. He writes extensively of the "new earth and new heaven" that Peter mentions (2 Peter 3:13, also in Isaiah 65:13), a place where justice reigns.

In this world, Luther says, sin reigns and we all are sinners. Given that we are, he argues that it is imperative that we have faith in Jesus, the salvation for our sinful state. Luther clearly establishes in his writing that salvation comes only and exclusively from a person's faith in Jesus. A person's works are inadequate, even irrelevant for achieving salvation since that would imply that God can be swayed or influenced by what we do. "No sin can separate us from Him, even if we were to kill or commit adultery thousands of times each day," Luther writes.[10] The magnitude of Jesus' sacrifice, his suffering and death, speaks, according to Luther, of the immensity of his salvation, regardless of our sins. Faith is the only path to salvation.

1. New Advent Catholic Encyclopedia, online at www.newadvent.com. It is acknowledged there that some scholars put his birth year at 1227 but that the consensus date is 1225. All of the biographical information here is found at the New Advent website article on Thomas Aquinas.

2. McBrien, 188.

3. Aquinas, 219.

4. ibid., 220.

5. ibid., 223.

6. ibid., 224.

7. ibid., 163.

8. ibid., 165.

9. Luther, 281.

10. Luther, 282

CHAPTER 8   WHERE WE DIFFER, WHAT WE SHARE REGARDING SIN AND EVIL

We all, Jews and Christians, start in the same place on the subject of sin and acts of evil, namely, that humans engage in sinful and evil behavior and that this phenomenon is a problem. Besides the problem that the sinful deeds can harm people, distance us from God, and destroy life, there is the fundamental theological problem. How can there be sin and evil in the human condition, in humans created by God if God is good, loving, and just? Why didn't God create humans to be good and decent and well-behaved, free of sin? As religious people, Christians and Jews, we have to confront the questions of the origin of sin and evil and God's possible role in that origin, how sin and evil are manifested in humans, and what we can do about it. As we might expect, there are similarities and differences between traditional Christianity and Judaism, as we have seen in the preceding chapters, regarding these religious issues.

Judaism, as reflected in the Bible and especially in the rabbinic literature, holds that God created humans with a capacity for evil.

In Genesis the earliest people sinned. As we saw above in Chapter 1, the word "sin" or in Hebrew, "*chet*," first appears in the Hebrew Bible in reference to the first humans, specifically, in the context of Cain's resentment of God's preference for Abel's offering. In the Jewish view, it was a resentment that led immediately and directly to an act of violence that constituted sin. As we read there in Genesis 4:7, "Sin couches at the door, its urge is toward you, yet you can be its master." Sin is ever present; it resides right there at the metaphoric entrance and exit to our homes and it has an urge toward us. We have the capacity to be the masters of the sinful urge, if we choose, by choosing to act rightly. By implication, we can also fail to master the urge and let it control us. God has given us the ability, the power to choose whether to manage and control the sinful urge or to submit to its power.

God is, according to the rabbinic literature, the One who implanted the evil inclination within us. The origin of sinfulness is not external, some force from the outside that corrupted humans, but a constitutional component of human nature. God wants us to have to struggle with the evil inclination, the urge to commit sin. Humans are born with the evil inclination and only develop the good inclination with which we can control the evil as we grow older. The evil inclination is always depicted as older and stronger than the wise, young, good inclination. God created us with an internal battlefield, and we are forced to try to master the sinfulness within that God implanted in us. In Talmud and Midrash there are no living humans who can expect to live without an evil inclination, who do not have to live with the struggle. The only people cited without an evil inclination are the righteous few of the Bible, the patriarchs and the select few like King David, Moses and Ezra. We might quibble over one example or the other, with David famously submitting to his evil inclination in the case of Bat Sheva and Moses submitting very differently when killing the Egyptian taskmaster beating the Hebrew slave. Despite these apparent lapses, and the rabbis have ways to explain them away, these men have become archetypes of humans who have, in a category all their own, transcended the power of the evil inclination.

According to the Jewish tradition, God wanted humans, all of us, to struggle to manage the evil inclination. The tradition also teaches that God provided the tools to strengthen the good inclination in its battle for supremacy. The problem is that the evil inclination is seen as older and stronger, as we have seen it depicted as an old king—a figure of power who has been around a long time. We are the battlefields for a difficult contest, possessing the good inclination that is always depicted as younger and weaker, though wiser. Left to our own devices, the odds are against us, so we need the laws God has given, the teachings of Torah, the practice of study and prayer, to have any chance of winning the battle. The rabbinic stories of sages who waged the battle and lost or barely won in a defining moment make it clear that all of us will lose from time to time; we will, episodically, succumb to the evil inclination.

The key, given that we will succumb to the evil inclination from time to time, is to make sure our sinful acts are as minor as possible. If we must stray, the rabbis tell us to do so where it will have minimal impact on others, in situations in which we will not persuade or lead others to sin. If we must sin along the way, the ideal is to do it in our thoughts and not in our actions, and if we must act, a private act is much preferred to a public act. What is amazing about this is the acknowledgment by the rabbinic tradition that we cannot expect to avoid the sinful behavior completely or permanently, we can expect at points along the way to succumb to the evil inclination. We might imagine it as a war in which battles will be won and lost and that the goal is to win the war, to live a life dominated by the good inclination.

The rabbis hold that the indispensable and necessary antidote to the evil inclination is the Torah and its laws. They repeatedly teach that when one feels drawn to the power of the evil inclination one should head immediately to the *bet midrash*, the house of study and prayer.

Prayer, the study of the laws of Torah and obedience to those laws will keep a person from sinning. Immersion in and obedience to God's laws are all that will keep a person from submitting to the evil inclination. We cannot expect to resist by sheer will power, and neither prayer nor faith alone will suffice to hold off the allures of the evil inclination. The very act of re-engaging with God's laws in Torah is all that will keep us from sinning. It is as if God provided the poison and the antidote—we already have the poison, the evil inclination, within us and God has given the antidote, the laws. We can decide if we want to employ the power of the antidote or leave it aside and let the poison run rampant, leading us directly to sin.

It is on this very question, the role of God's laws as they relate to our inclination to sin, that we find the most profound difference between the teaching of Paul in the New Testament and that of the rabbis in the rabbinic literature. Paul argues in Romans that while Adam's violation of God's command prohibiting the eating of the fruit of the tree of the knowledge of good and evil introduced sin into the world (more on Original Sin below), sin expanded its reach when Moses gave the law. Paul holds that it is law itself that incites people to sin. If there were not laws against, for instance, adultery, people would not commit adultery, according to Paul. Laws prohibiting acts encourage people to commit the acts.

On one level, this can seem consistent with the rabbinic teaching cited above that holds that people are tempted to engage in prohibited acts just because we are drawn to do that which is prohibited. The rabbis use the example of Rabbi Haggai who was sick on Yom Kippur; when he is told that due to his illness he can drink, he loses his thirst. He wanted to drink because it was prohibited and loses the desire when it is permitted. While the rabbis and Paul would agree that people want to do that which is prohibited, there is a radical difference between the rabbis and Paul on the function of the laws of Torah generally. The rabbis hold that the law is the only thing that keeps us from sinning. It is this difference that contributed mightily to the parting of the ways between Paul and his companions in the nascent movement of Jesus adherents and the rest of the Jewish community. While Paul argues that the law given by Moses causes people to sin, the rabbis hold just the opposite. Returning to our example of the ill and thirsty Rabbi Haggai on Yom Kippur, the rabbis would hold that the prohibition against drinking made him thirsty, and that it was the law itself that kept him from acting on the desire. People may want to do the prohibited, but it is God's law that keeps us from actually doing the prohibited. Agreement on the question of the enticing power of the prohibited act should not distract us from the fundamental difference between the position of Paul and the rabbinic tradition on the question of the role of law in the realm of sin and human evil.

Paul cites Adam's act of disobedience in eating the prohibited fruit as the singular act that introduces sin into the world. Sin did not exist before that act. That means that humans, specifically the first humans, existed without the presence of sin in the moments before they ate the prohibited fruit. While he does not call this idea Original Sin, it is the kernel of the idea that Augustine develops over three hundred years later. Paul's idea was a new one and one not supported by existing Jewish writings, at least ones that have survived. Where the rabbis subsequently taught that God implanted the evil inclination within us in our moment of creation, Paul holds that sinfulness does not appear until a human willfully disobeys God.

It is this teaching of Paul that becomes the foundation for the traditional Christian doctrine of Original Sin. Original Sin is the key, often the misunderstood key, to the Christian concept of human nature and our tendency to commit sin. While Paul lays down in his writings that are canonized in the New Testament what becomes the foundation of the doctrine, it only becomes a clear doctrinal idea in the writings of Augustine. Augustine builds on Paul's theological foundation and creates the doctrine of Original Sin as it becomes known in Christian (although not Eastern Orthodox Christianity) tradition. There is no uniformity of understanding across Christian teachings on the precise concept of Original Sin, although it generally can be understood as the idea that all humans inherit, as a result of Adam's "fall" in his decision to eat the forbidden fruit, a sinful character, a distance from God. Each person still has to decide whether to commit his or her own personal sins, but the lack of holiness we understand as Original Sin resides in the human spirit.

It is not our purpose here to explore the intriguing issues of how baptism works in relation to Original Sin or to look into the differences between Roman Catholic and Protestant teachings on the subject. We are interested in how the idea of Original Sin differentiates Christian teachings on the question of human sinfulness from that of Judaism. Because Judaism never uses the language of Original Sin and does not associate sinfulness with the act of Adam and Eve, the tendency is to see a dramatic difference between the two faith traditions on the subject. Surely there is a theological difference between the rabbinic teaching that God implanted an evil inclination in humans and Augustine's teaching that God created man as good and that sinfulness was introduced into the human condition by Adam's disobedient act. Judaism believes God created man with an internal inclination to sin, and Christianity, in the idea of Original Sin, holds that man was created good and stumbled into sinfulness by a willful act. Either sin is internal and inherent or sin is external to humans introduced by a human act.

Judaism and Christianity do not see the origin of sinfulness in the same way. But the result is essentially the same, especially in practical rather than theological terms. Whether sin is inherent or external in origin, both traditions understand that every human has an inclination to sin, an internal compass that orients us toward sinning. Both traditions hold that each human has to decide whether to succumb to that inclination, that character, or to try to resist. In both cases each person must choose whether to sin or not. Whether God originally created man as fundamentally good, as traditional Christian teachings hold or God created man with an evil inclination and good inclination as traditional Jewish teachings hold, the end result is the same. Each of us has to decide whether, when, how and how much to sin.

Both Judaism and Christianity have much to say about what constitutes sin, how it is manifested in the human experience. As we have seen, Judaism begins its discussion of sin with the story of Cain and Abel, a brother's resentment that led to the first act of violence. Physical aggression and violence are recurring themes in the Jewish and subsequently Christian perception of the evil inclination and sin. One difference between the two faith traditions on the manifestation of sin and evil is the Jewish focus on idolatry. By the time the rabbis of the rabbinic literature are discussing the evil inclination and its influence on human behavior they recognized that idolatry was no longer a significant problem for Jews. In discussing the evil inclination in Biblical terms they make clear, especially using the example of the Golden Calf incident in Exodus, that it is the evil inclination that leads people to engage in acts of idolatry. The rabbis believe that by their time the issue of idolatry has been resolved and that acts of illicit sexual behavior, physical aggression and violence are the dominant concerns when considering sinful behavior. Christian tradition also focuses on sexual behavior and violence as the dominant manifestations of sin in humans. In both traditions it is this behavior above others that distances people from God and thus constitutes sin.

Another fundamental difference between traditional Christian and Jewish thought on the topic of sin is the question of the role of physicality, especially as it appears in the writings of Augustine. As we saw, the bishop of Hippo wrote extensively about the dichotomy of body and soul, between the physical and the spiritual. He sees the pursuit of the physical, the pursuit of material desires and pleasures as the root of sin. A person cannot completely deny the physical and the body itself is not a source of sin since it was created by God, but Augustine holds that it is in the focus on or pursuit of the desires of the body that one inevitably commits sin. We do not see any similar teaching in the writings of the rabbis and in fact, typically the opposite. The rabbis do not recognize such a stark dichotomy between the physical and the spiritual and they do not see material desires themselves as a cause of sin. The rabbis hold that the desires of the body, when exercised in moderation, are an appreciation of the gifts and blessings of a bountiful and merciful God. Where the rabbis and Augustine would agree, in this question of the dangers of physical desires, is that moderation is the key to goodness and the avoidance of sin.

As we will see below in the appendix, the Roman Catholic Church developed the idea of categories of sin, specifically, mortal, venial, and serious. This helps people to understand the dimensions and relative severity of the sins in which we engage. Judaism never tries to create such a hierarchy or set of formal categories. In fact, the rabbinic tradition warns against making our own decisions about which transgressions of God's laws are more serious. As soon as we do that we open the door, the rabbis would say, to decide which transgressions are acceptable and which are not. In both Jewish and Christian tradition the imagery of archery is used to understand sin. Both traditions adopt the language of "missing the mark" to understand what constitutes sin. When our behavior misses the mark of what we want for ourselves and what God wants for us we have engaged in sin.

There is agreement and disagreement between Jewish and Christian doctrine on the issues explored in these pages. I believe that the areas of agreement outweigh those of disagreement. How God created man is purely a theological issue, of interest primarily to people who ponder such imponderables. What matters is how we see humans in practical terms, what is the responsibility of each human. Neither tradition holds that we are compelled to sin and both hold that we will, being human, inevitably sin. Our character, even in the doctrine of Original Sin, does not force us to engage in sinful acts. We are forced to choose whether to sin and our humanity includes the necessary conclusion that we will sin to varying degrees and amounts. Each of us can control what sins we commit, the severity and damage of the sins we commit and the frequency of our sinning.

We arrive at the question that forms the title of the book: Are we sinners? The question is purposely vague and cryptic. If the commission of a sin makes us sinners, then both Judaism and Christianity hold that we are. If the question asks whether we humans are characterologically sinful beings, creations of God who are compelled to sin, both Judaism and Christianity would answer in the negative. I can choose to be good even though I will inevitably stumble and sin along the way. We are beings with the capacity to sin, and our freely chosen acts determine our moral character. We shape our moral character by the free choices we make every day. Each person determines the extent to which he or she is a sinner and so each of us answers in the choosing moments of our lives whether we are sinners.

My personal and professional quest over the last thirty years of my adult life and professional career as a rabbi has been to plumb the similarities and differences between the Judaism of my ancestral heritage and personal life and the Christianity of the society into which I was born. I grew up with the idea that Judaism and Christianity are profoundly different on any number of topics. One of my clearest memories of my religious school teaching at the local synagogue where I grew up in Los Angeles was the teacher's insight that "Christians read the Bible, Jews study it." This and myriad other observations, prejudices and insights formed my conceptualization of Judaism and Christianity as radically different on most religious topics. That understanding began to crumble when I became a rabbi and functioned in a small New England town as the only rabbi of the only synagogue. I spent much of my time as a rabbi interacting with the local priests, ministers and pastors talking about our respective work and our beliefs. While always mindful of the seminal differences I became struck with the areas of similarity both in our work and in our faith. Our idea of the messiah was different, our belief about salvation was different and other differences remained clear. But increasingly it became clear to me that we had similar ideas about our relationship to God, our understanding of what constitutes moral behavior and even our idea of what constitutes sin.

In my teaching, now primarily about Judaism to Christians, I am careful to emphasize my belief that to forge a new relationship of mutual acceptance, even one of love, that we must be mindful of both our similarities and our differences. In the subject at hand in these pages, I believe we are focused on a topic in which our similarities outweigh our differences. The differences are superficial or theoretical. Original Sin is an important concept in Christian theology and it does not exist in Judaism. But as I have pointed out, we end up in the same place. Humans exist in a perpetual state of moral choice, a state in which we have the freedom and the responsibility to create our own moral condition. Are we sinners? Judaism and Christianity both teach that we have to decide through the choices we make every day throughout our lives. We will determine whether we are sinners or not. Are we sinners in those moments when we choose to sin or do we become sinners as a result of a pattern of repeated sinful behavior? I will leave the answer to that question in the hands, mind and faith of the reader.

APPENDIX   MORTAL, VENIAL, SERIOUS SIN AND THE SACRAMENT OF PENANCE

The Catholic Church defines three categories of sin that are relevant to our discussion here: mortal, serious and venial. Mortal sin is a fundamental rejection of God and it fully consumes the person committing it. Mortal sin leads inevitably toward choices that shape us as a person. Venial sin is understood to be a sin that is inconsistent with our normative orientation toward God. It constitutes a decision to commit a certain act, but not to change who we are fundamentally as people. In venial sin a person will choose a certain act, but not repeat it so that it would become a pattern. It is understood that the person who commits a venial sin still wants to be a good person in relationship with God. There is inherently a contradiction between the person and the act. Serious sin is, well, more serious than venial sin, but not the same as mortal sin. While a venial sin may be trivial and not terribly consequential, a serious sin is weighty and quite significant. It does not fully engage a person like the mortal sin does, but it is certainly something worth noting in a person's conduct.

The Church offers the sacrament of Penance as a response to the commission of sins. In the New Testament Jesus and the apostles are extensively recorded as willing to provide forgiveness for people's sins. Penance became one of the seven sacraments of the Church over the centuries and the rite was revised as recently as the Second Vatican Council in 1965. In that document it is declared that the purpose of the sacrament is to "obtain pardon from the mercy of God" and to be "reconciled with the Church whom (sinners) have wounded by their sin." Confession is a key element of the sacrament, and since Vatican II confession is primarily a public, communal act rather than a private one.

Bibliography

Chesterton, G.K., *St. Thomas Aquinas, St. Francis Assisi*, Ignatius Press, San Francisco CA, 1933.

Davies, Brian, ed., *Martin Luther,* Oxford University Press, Oxford, 2002

Holy Bible, New Revised Standard Version, Thomas Nelson Publishers, Nashville TN, 1990

Davies, Brian, ed., *Thomas Aquinas,* Oxford University Press, Oxford, 2002

Luther, Martin, *Reformation Writings* (translated and edited), Lutterworth Press, London, 1952.

McBride, Richard P., *Catholicism*, Harper San Francisco, 1994.

Rigby, Paul, *Original Sin in Augustine's Confessions*, University of Ottawa Press, Ottawa, 1987

Saint Augustine, *The City of God*, translated by Marcus Dods, D.D., The Modern Library, NY, 1950.

Saint Thomas Aquinas, *Aquinas's Shorter Summa*, Sophia Institute Press, Manchester, NH 1993.

Sheed, F.J., translator, *The Confessions of St. Augustine*, Sheed & Ward, NY, 1943

Snell, Sr. Roberta (dissertation), *The Nature of Man in St. Thomas Aquinas Compared with the Nature of Man in American Sociology*, Catholic University of America Press, Washington DC, 1942

"Summa Theologica," in New Advent Catholic Encyclopedia online, newadvent.org/summa

Rabbinic Sources Cited

Babylonian Talmud

Berachot 5a, 17a, 20a, 54a, 60b, 61ab, 63b

Sukkah 52a

Sanhedrin 39a, 43b, 91b, 99b,105a

Nedarim 32ab

Chagigah 16ab

Shabbat 62b, 63b, 89a, 105b

Yoma 9b

Sotah 8a

Kiddushin 21b, 30b, 81b

Niddah 13b

Baba Batra 16a, 17a

Baba Metzia 32b

Temurah 16b

Avot 2:11, 4:1, 22

Avot d'Rabi Natan 3, 16, 20, 32

Jerusalem Talmud

Berachot 3.6d, 4.7d, 9.12d, 9.14b

Shabbat 14.14c

Yoma 6.43d

Sukkah 5.55b

Ta'anit 3.66c

Sotah 3.18c

Kiddushin 4.66b

Midrash

Bereshit (Genesis) Rabbah 9.7, 14.4, 22.6, 27.4, 34.10, 48.11, 53.10, 54.1, 67.8, 70.8, 89.1

Shemot (Exodus) Rabbah 15.6, 30.17, 35.5, 36.3, 41.7, 46.4,

Vayikra (Leviticus) Rabbah 16.8, 23.11, 34.1, 35.5

Bamidbar (Numbers) Rabbah 15.14, 17.6, 19.5

Devarim (Deuteronomy) Rabbah 2.30, 6.14

Shir Hashirim (Song of Songs) Rabbah 1:2.4, 2:4.1, 4:4.1, 4:4.3, 7:8.1, 7:11.1

Kohelet (Ecclesiastes) Rabbah 3:3, 4:8.1, 4:13.1, 4:16.1, 9:2, 9:7.1, 9:14.6

Pesikta deRav Kahana 4:6, 11:1, 23:7, 24:17, 3(supplement)

Tanhuma Bereshit (Genesis) 1:38, 1:40, 2:13, 3:19, 11:1; 7 (Warsaw ed.)

Shemot (Exodus) 3:16, 4:1

Bamidbar (Numbers) 3:15, 6:1

Tehillim (Psalms) Rabbah 14:1, 16:2, 31:5, 41:1, 57:1, 119:7, 119:64

Mishlei (Proverbs) Rabbah 11:21

Tosefta Baba Kamah 9:31

Printed in the United States
by Baker & Taylor Publisher Services